ManageFirst®
Customer Service
Competency Guide

D1614009

Upper Saddle River, New Jersey 07458

Disclaimer

Requests for permission to use or reproduce material from this book should be directed to:

Copyright Permissions
National Restaurant Association Solutions
175 West Jackson Boulevard, Suite 1500
Chicago, IL 60604-2814
Email: permissions@restaurant.org

ManageFirst® and ManageFirst Professional® are registered trademarks and ManageFirst Program™ and MFP™ are trademarks of the National Restaurant Association Educational Foundation and used under license by National Restaurant Association Solutions, LLC, a wholly owned subsidiary of the National Restaurant Association.

ISBN: 978-0-13-228381-6 (Competency Guide with Examination Answer Sheet)

Printed in the U.S.A.

10 9 8 7

Table of Contents

A Message from the National Restaurant Association

Founded in 1919, the National Restaurant Association is the leading business association for the restaurant industry. Together with the National Restaurant Association Educational Foundation (NRAEF) and National Restaurant Association Solutions (NRA Solutions) our goal is to lead America's restaurant industry into a new era of prosperity, prominence, and participation, enhancing the quality of life for all we serve.

As one of the nation's largest private-sector employers, the restaurant, hospitality and foodservice industry is the cornerstone of the American economy, of career-and-employment opportunities, and of local communities. The overall impact of the restaurant industry is astounding. The restaurant industry is expected to add 1.8 million jobs over the next decade, with employment reaching 14.8 million by 2019. At the National Restaurant Association, we are focused on enhancing this position by providing the valuable tools and resources needed to educate our current and future professionals.

For more information on the National Restaurant Association, please visit our Web site at www.restaurant.org.

What Is the ManageFirst Program™?

The ManageFirst Program is a management-training certificate program that exemplifies our commitment to developing materials by the industry, for the industry. The program's most powerful strength is that it is based on a set of competencies defined by the restaurant, foodservice, and hospitality industry as critical for success. For more information on the ManageFirst Program, visit www.managefirst.restaurant.org.

ManageFirst Program Components

The ManageFirst Program includes a set of Competency Guides, exams, Instructor Resources, certificates, a credential, and support activities and services. By participating in the program, you are demonstrating your commitment to becoming a highly qualified professional preparing either to begin or to advance your career in the restaurant, hospitality, and foodservice industry.

The Competency Guides cover the range of topics listed in the chart at right.

Competency Guide/Exam Topics

ManageFirst Core Credential Topics

Controlling Foodservice Costs

Hospitality and Restaurant Management

Human Resources Management and Supervision

ServSafe® Food Safety

ManageFirst Elective Topics

Customer Service

Food Production

Inventory and Purchasing

Managerial Accounting

Menu Marketing and Management

Nutrition

Restaurant Marketing

ServSafe Alcohol® Responsible Alcohol Service

Within the guides, you will find the essential content for the topic as defined by industry, as well as learning activities, assessments, case studies, suggested field projects, professional profiles, and testimonials. You can also find an answer sheet or an online exam voucher for a NRA Solutions exam written specifically for each topic. The exam can be administered either online or in a paper and pencil format (see inside front cover for a listing of ISBNs), and it will be proctored. Upon successfully passing the exam, you will be issued a customized certificate from NRA Solutions. The certificate is a lasting recognition of your accomplishment and a signal to the industry that you have mastered the competency covered within the particular topic.

To earn the ManageFirst Professional™ (MFP™) credential, you will be required to pass four core exams and one elective exam (to be chosen from the remaining program topics) and to document your work experience in the restaurant and foodservice industry. Earning the MFP credential is a significant accomplishment.

We applaud you as you either begin or advance your career in the restaurant, hospitality, and foodservice industry. Visit *www.managefirst.restaurant.org* to learn about additional career-building resources offered through the National Restaurant Association, including scholarships for college students enrolled in relevant industry programs.

ManageFirst Program Ordering Information

Review copies or support materials:
FACULTY FIELD SERVICES

Domestic orders and inquiries:
PEARSON CUSTOMER SERVICE
Tel: 800.922.0579

International orders and inquiries:
U.S. EXPORT SALES OFFICE
Pearson Education International Customer Service Group
200 Old Tappan Road
Old Tappan, NJ 07675 USA
Tel: 201.767.5021

For corporate, government, and special sales (consultants, corporations, training centers, VARs, and corporate resellers) orders and inquiries:
PEARSON CORPORATE SALES
Tel: 317.428.3411
Fax: 317.428.3343

For additional information regarding other Prentice Hall publications, instructor and student support materials, locating your sales representative, and much more, please visit *www.prenhall.com/managefirst*.

Acknowledgements

The National Restaurant Association Solutions is grateful for the significant contributions made to this competency guide by the following individuals.

John A. Hart

In addition, we are pleased to thank our many other advisors, subject matter experts, reviewers, and contributors for their time, effort, and dedication to this program.

Teresa Marie Gargano Adamski

Ernest Boger

Robert Bosselman

Jerald Chesser

Cynthia Deale

Fred DeMicco

Johnathan Deustch

John Drysdale

Gene Fritz

John Gescheidle

Thomas Hamilton

Ray Kavanaugh

John Kidwell

Carol Kizer

Holly Ruttan Maloney

Cynthia Mayo

Fred Mayo

Patrick Moreo

Robert O'Halloran

Brian O'Malley

Terrence Pappas

James Perry

Patricia Plavcan

William N. Reynolds

Rosenthal Group

Mokie Steiskal

Karl Titz

Terry Umbreit

David Wightman

Deanne Williams

Mike Zema

Renee Zonka

Features of the ManageFirst Competency Guides®

We have designed the ManageFirst competency guides to enhance your ability to learn and retain important information that is critical to this restaurant and foodservice industry function. Here are the key features you will find within this guide.

Beginning Each Guide

Tuning In to You

When you open a ManageFirst competency guide for the first time, you might ask yourself: Why do I need to know about this topic? Every topic of these guides involves key information you will need as you manage a restaurant or foodservice operation. Located in the front of each review guide, "Tuning In to You" is a brief synopsis that illustrates some of the reasons the information contained throughout that particular guide is important to you. It exemplifies real-life scenarios that you will face as a manager and how the concepts in the book will help you in your career.

Professional Profile

This is your opportunity to meet a professional who is currently working in the field associated with a competency guide's topic. This person's story will help you gain insight into the responsibilities related to his or her position, as well as the training and educational history linked to it. You will also see the daily and cumulative impact this position has on an operation, and receive advice from a person who has successfully met the challenges of being a manager.

Beginning Each Chapter

Inside This Chapter

Chapter content is organized under these major headings.

Learning Objectives

Learning objectives identify what you should be able to do after completing each chapter. These objectives are linked to the required tasks a manager must be able to perform in relation to the function discussed in the competency guide.

Test Your Knowledge

Each chapter begins with some True or False questions designed to test your prior knowledge of some of the concepts presented in the chapter. The answers to these questions, as well as the concepts behind them, can be found within the chapter—see the page reference after each question.

Key Terms

These terms are important for thorough understanding of the chapter's content. They are highlighted throughout the chapter, where they are explicitly defined or their meaning is made clear within the paragraphs in which they appear.

Throughout Each Chapter

Exhibits

Exhibits are placed throughout each chapter to visually reinforce the key concepts presented in the text. Types of exhibits include charts, tables, photographs, and illustrations.

Think About It...

These thought-provoking sidebars reveal supportive information about the section they appear beside.

Activities

Apply what you have learned throughout the chapter by completing the various activities in the text. The activities have been designed to give you additional practice and better understanding of the concepts addressed in the learning objectives. Types of activities include case study, role-play, and problem solving, among others.

Exhibit

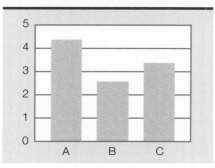

Exhibits are visuals that will help you learn about key concepts.

Think About It...

Consider these supplemental insights as you read through a chapter.

Activity

Activity

Types of activities you will complete include case study, role-play, and problem solving, among others.

At the End of Each Chapter

Review Your Learning

These multiple-choice or open- or close-ended questions or problems are designed to test your knowledge of the concepts presented in the chapter. These questions have been aligned with the objectives and should provide you with an opportunity to practice or apply the content that supports these objectives. If you have difficulty answering them, you should review the content further.

At the End of the Guide

Field Project

This real-world project gives you the valuable opportunity to apply many of the concepts you will learn in a competency guide. You will interact with industry practitioners, enhance your knowledge, and research, apply, analyze, evaluate, and report on your findings. It will provide you with an in-depth "reality check" of the policies and practices of this management function.

Tuning In to You

As a manager of a restaurant or foodservice establishment, one of your main goals is to be profitable. A lot of your energy may be spent looking for new ways to do this, from cutting costs to improving your business's image. A critical aspect of being profitable is your ability to provide high-quality customer service to every member of your operation, including guests and employees.

Customer service is often overlooked as an important element of a profitable restaurant or foodservice business. But the quality of service to a customer impacts every part of the operation. Customers are not just those who dine at your establishment, they are also your employees. Satisfying both is important in the success of your business. Understanding the complex relationship between your customers and your operation is a significant goal you as a manager should strive for.

The service-profit chain is one way of looking at the relationship between an establishment and the customers it serves. The chain begins with internal service quality, which means that your establishment provides the services employees need to do their job well. Once employees are satisfied with the services your operation provides them, they will be more likely to remain with the operation and do their jobs well. Because your internal customers provide services to your external customers, the satisfaction of internal customers is necessary. Internal customers, your employees, set the stage for the experience external customers will have at your operation.

Knowing how to better provide for and anticipate your guests' expectations will better prepare you to satisfy them. Meeting or exceeding customer expectations creates a base of customers who know how important they are to your operation and who are more likely to return. External customers who are satisfied will be loyal, and they are more likely to spread the word about the service they receive at your establishment. In the end, the relationship you develop with your customers reduces your expenses. You will spend less money on hiring and training new employees because your internal customers will remain at your restaurant or foodservice operation. You will also gain free advertising through your external customers who are eager to share their experience, and the additional customers you get will increase your revenue.

The knowledge of providing customer satisfaction can be learned, and this guide will show you how to attain it. Because customers drive the profitability of your business, providing satisfaction is an important part of your role as a manager. What is more, the high-quality service you and your operation provide to your customers will ultimately bring satisfaction to you as well.

Professional Profile

Your opportunity to meet someone working in the field

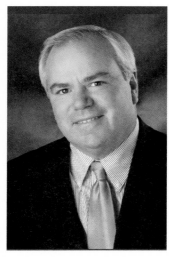

Craig C. Culver

CEO and Cofounder
Culver Franchising System, Inc.
Prairie du Sac, WI

This mission statement appears in every Culver's restaurant: "Every guest who chooses Culver's leaves happy." I am the CEO and cofounder of Culver Franchising System Inc., a quick-service operation with more than three hundred units in fifteen states.

Along with my wife, Lea, and parents George and Ruth Culver, I took a vision and created a successful niche-market restaurant chain featuring burgers and frozen custard. By wearing several hats, I have built my career through a commitment to doing what is right for my guests, team members, franchisees, and family.

I have deep roots in Sauk City, Wisconsin, the small Sauk Prairie community where I grew up. For well over three decades, my family owned and operated several supper clubs in the Sauk Prairie area. During college breaks, I worked at the Farm Kitchen Resort doing many different jobs, which is where I met my future wife, Lea Weiss.

After graduating from the University of Wisconsin Oshkosh with a biology degree, I went to work for McDonald's Corporation. In my four years there, I learned about consistency and the operations of multiple locations.

In Sauk City, a root-beer stand provided the foundation for the Culver's concept—which is where my family and I opened the first Culver's on July 18, 1984. In 1987, the franchising arm, Culver Franchising System Inc. (CFSI), was established, and the first successful franchise was opened in Baraboo, Wisconsin in 1990.

CFSI practices the internal/external customer philosophy. The owner/operator concept is a key factor in the success of CFSI. Its belief that locally owned and operated restaurants ensure the highest-quality customer service has proven successful many times. Culver's restaurants are the benchmark for high-quality products and high-quality customer service in their market niche.

Not just anyone can purchase a Culver's franchise. "We don't sell franchises, we award them," is my reply when asked about franchising possibilities. Before being awarded a franchise, candidates have to complete an intense sixteen-week training program in which they are taught the technical aspects of operating a Culver's franchise. During this training, the candidates' people skills, passion, and commitment are also scrutinized. If a candidate fails to meet Culver's standards, the franchise will not be awarded. This process is a key factor for ensuring the consistency of high-quality customer service and products throughout the Culver's system.

I explain it this way: "Leaders set the example. Our owner/operators are the leaders in the restaurant. The example they set is modeled by their team." To that end, I am insistent on finding potential franchisees who share my business philosophy and who are committed to put into practice the Culver's mission statement. Culver's reputation for having a solid business concept and our commitment to high-quality customer service have attracted high-quality team members at all levels of the Culver's organization.

Following is my advice for graduates of a hotel/restaurant management program:

1 **Find a mentor.** Look for a proven leader within the organization—someone who is willing to guide you through the maze of starting a career on the right foot. You should ideally seek a person who can become an advisor when you begin your own initiatives.

2 **Get a variety of experiences.** For an entry-level opportunity, apply for work at an organization that shares your business philosophy and provides a variety of work experiences. Some organizations limit the management responsibilities of entry-level managers, so look for organizations with established management training programs. When the training is complete, the manager trainee is given the responsibility and authority to make decisions and solve problems.

3 **Find your passion.** If you do not have passion for what you are doing, work will become drudgery. I am proud of saying, "At Culver's we don't say we're going to work. We say we're going to play." Every day is not going to be perfect—there are going to be days when it seems that nothing is working out. Without passion for what you are doing, those times will become unbearable and will seem to happen more frequently.

4 **Seek a team of great people.** Successful people help other people succeed. Read industry publications such as *Nation's Restaurant News* to discover the businesses that people are talking positively about. Do research on these organizations and study their annual reports. When you find yourself in a position to make hiring decisions, make the right choice, not the convenient choice.

As CEO, I am actively involved as a coach, cheerleader, and mentor to all franchisees and their teams. I frequently visit Culver's restaurants throughout the system to show my appreciation for each team's hard work and dedication. I am also concerned with food safety—I have nationally certified ServSafe instructors on staff, and my goal is to go beyond state and federal standards. I am supportive of the agricultural community as well, including the "Eat More Pork" campaign to raise awareness of low pork prices, and the "Drink More Milk" campaign with similar pricing and supply issues. I believe that high-quality ingredients and family-owned businesses go hand in hand.

CFSI encourages our franchisees to be good citizens in the communities they serve. At the CFSI Annual Conference, awards and recognition are given to the owner/operators for outstanding contributions in community service as well as achieving business goals. My wife has led by example and helped set the standard for community involvement. Under our leadership, the Culver's VIP Foundation was established, which awards over $100,000 a year in scholarship funds for Culver's team members to continue their education. The foundation also provides financial support to a variety of not-for-profit organizations.

In addition to serving on the board of the Culver's VIP Foundation, I am also a board member of the UW Oshkosh Foundation, the Bank of Prairie du Sac, Lutheran Social Services, American Family Insurance, and the Wisconsin Historical Society, and a member of the National Restaurant Association and the Wisconsin Restaurant Association.

The Importance of Customer Service to Your Business

1

Inside This Chapter

- What the Customer Buys
- What Is Customer Service?
- Impact of Customer Service
- Making a Positive Impression
- Completing the Cycle

After completing this chapter, you should be able to:

- Explain the importance of customer service to a restaurant or foodservice operation.
- Differentiate between hospitality and service.
- List and explain the impact of customer service.
- Identify the relationship between customer satisfaction and customer loyalty.
- Define moments of truth.
- Identify the cycle of service.

Test Your Knowledge

1 True or False: It is possible to have poor hospitality but good service. *(See p. 5.)*

2 True or False: Having a good product gives you enough of a competitive advantage. *(See p. 5.)*

3 True or False: Higher profits are a result of higher levels of service. *(See p. 9.)*

4 True or False: Customer loyalty is a result of good customer service. *(See p. 10.)*

5 True or False: The customer buys an entire dining experience. *(See p. 4.)*

6 True or False: Speed and organization in the operation, as well as the attitude of employees, are all part of high-quality customer service. *(See pp. 6–7.)*

7 True or False: Poor customer service can lead to employee turnover. *(See p. 11.)*

8 True or False: The customer's "cycle of service" begins when he or she enters the establishment. *(See pp. 14–15.)*

9 True or False: "Moments of truth" for a dining experience can only happen during the meal. *(See p. 14.)*

Key Terms

Competitive point of difference

Cost-benefit ratio

Customer loyalty

Cycle of service

High-quality customer service

Hospitality

Moment of truth

Process

Service

Standard

System

Task

Think About It...

What is more important to the consumer; the quality of the product or the quality of the service? Which has the most impact on customer loyalty?

Introduction

Everyone talks about providing or receiving good customer service. But what is good customer service? To some people in the restaurant industry, serving hot food hot and cold food cold represents good customer service. But good customer service is more than that. The hot food must be the correct item ordered, served promptly to the correct guest, and in a pleasant manner. (See *Exhibit 1a.*) To achieve this, you should have proper policies, procedures, systems, and people in place.

Exhibit 1a

Good customer service involves more than just serving hot food hot, or cold food cold.

There are many benefits to providing good customer service in your operation. They include:

- Increased customer satisfaction
- Increased customer loyalty
- Decreased marketing expenditures
- Enhanced business reputation
- Reduced employee turnover
- Increased profits

In the following chapters, you will explore ways to achieve good-quality customer service.

Activity

How Would You Define Customer Service?

1. Think of a restaurant or foodservice experience where you received the poorest customer service. Describe what made it so poor.

2. Think of the restaurant or foodservice experience in which you received the best customer service. Describe what made it the best.

3. Based on all your restaurant or foodservice experiences, describe what makes customer service excellent for you.

4. Reverse the viewpoint and describe what providing excellent customer service means to a restaurant or foodservice employee, such as a server.

What the Customer Buys

When customers patronize your restaurant or foodservice operation, they purchase three distinct items (see *Exhibit 1b*):

- ■ Products
- ■ Service
- ■ Dining experience

First, they purchase products to consume, such as entrées, side dishes, beverages, and desserts. To have satisfied customers, the products must meet the expectations for the type of restaurant or foodservice operation they are served in. If they do not meet the customer's expectations, the dining experience will be negative and difficult to save. However, excellent customer service can turn a negative experience into a positive one.

Customers also purchase service when they dine out. The level and nature of the service varies widely from quick-service establishments to fine-dining establishments. Customers have service expectations from each type of establishment, and they make a conscious decision to buy that type of service when they visit that type of establishment. Along with products, service must also measure up to the customer's standards. If service does not measure up, the dining experience will be negative—even if the product was excellent.

Finally, customers also purchase a total dining experience when they visit a restaurant or foodservice establishment. This experience consists of the products and service, the theme, image, ambience, prices charged, any entertainment, and other factors. All of these factors must work together to create a positive, and hopefully, an excellent experience for the customer. When this happens, the customer is satisfied and recommends the establishment to others.

Exhibit 1b

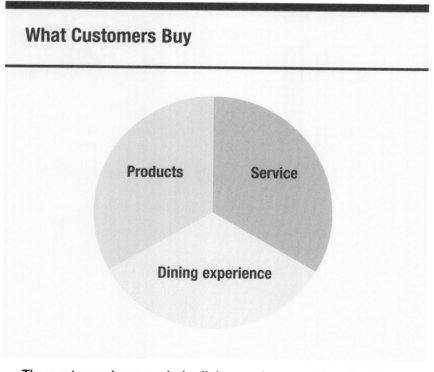

What Customers Buy

Products

Service

Dining experience

The customer buys a whole dining package, not just food.

When an establishment does not meet the customer's minimum expectations, the customer will probably have negative things to say about the establishment.

What Is Customer Service?

Customer service often makes the difference between positive or excellent dining experiences and negative or ordinary ones. In fact, products served by similar competitive restaurants are usually very much alike and do not add much of a competitive advantage. The competitive advantage comes from the nature and quality of customer service. It is therefore important for every type of operation to provide the best possible level of customer service to stand out from the competition.

This chapter examines what is involved in providing good customer service. It also provides a definition of customer service that can be implemented in your operation.

Hospitality Versus Service

Recently, a golf championship was played at a course in Wisconsin. A few months later, the golf organization announced the return of the tournament to that same course in five and ten years with a major tournament in fifteen years. One of the deciding factors was the hospitality provided by the staff at the golf course and its restaurant, and by the people of the town and county. (See *Exhibit 1c.*)

Service is *what* restaurant and foodservice employees provide; it is a measure of the efficiency and effectiveness of their actions. **Hospitality** is *how* services are performed; it is the feeling that customers take with them. Hospitality and service are critical for high-quality customer service.

Exhibit 1c

Superb customer service, including hospitality, can help gain long-term customer loyalty.

Activity

Providing Customer Service

Imagine you are the dining room manager of a fine-dining restaurant. You observe two employees seating guests on the same evening in the same time period. The following is a description of what you observe.

1 *Employee #1*

"Good evening. How many? Follow me." The employee races to the table, leaving the guests to catch up. "Here you go. Your server will be with you shortly."

2 *Employee #2*

"Good evening, Mr. and Mrs. Jones! Will there be just you two this evening?" (The employee notices that the couple is dressed more formally than usual.) "Are you celebrating a special occasion? Well, happy anniversary. I'll try to find you a quiet table. Would you follow me, please?" The employee carefully leads the couple to a table. "Here we are. I think you will like this table. Steven will be your server tonight and will be with you shortly. Happy anniversary, and enjoy your evening."

Employee #1 and Employee #2 both did their jobs: the guests were greeted and seated. Which of these two employees provided better customer service? If you were the dining room manager, which of these scenarios would you prefer your staff to copy? Why?

_____

_____

_____

_____

High-Quality Customer Service

Recall that the level of customer service provided is a major factor that sets apart competing establishments. Therefore, the higher the quality of customer service, the better for the establishment and customer. **High-quality customer service** means consistently exceeding customers' expectations for products and the nature of services received, and for personal interaction during the delivery, to create value for the customer and profit for the organization.

■ **Nature of service** includes things such as timeliness, speed, organization, smoothness or efficiency, uniformity, correctness, convenience, correction of mistakes, etc. In other words, the nature of service includes what you do and how well you do it.

■ **Personal interactions during service delivery** include things such as attitude, friendliness, sensitivity to a situation or individual needs, interest in the customer, tactfulness, discretion, avoiding embarrassment, privacy protection, complaint and difficult situation management, etc. In other words, it includes how you treat people when you provide service.

To provide high-quality customer service, you must do well at both service delivery and personal interaction. Doing just one or the other is not enough. The concept of high-quality customer service will continue to be expanded in the following chapters of this book.

You Must Keep Improving

Achieving high-quality customer service is a process that needs continuous improvement. Even though things are going well at the operation, you should not assume that there is no room for improvement. Even when things go smoothly, ask yourself, "How can we provide better service to our customers? What process could be improved? What system can we run more smoothly?"

Customer Service Systems, Processes, and Tasks

To create high-quality customer service, you should have systems and processes in place; to make sure products and services are consistent, you must manage those systems. A **system** is a set of standards, processes, and tasks that work together in an organized way to achieve an end result. (See *Exhibit 1d.*)

Your operation should have well-defined standards for the business. A **standard** describes criteria for items, tasks, behaviors, practices, and other aspects of an operation that represent the norm for your business. For example, you may have standards for cleanliness that specify all silverware must be spot-free. Another establishment may have a service standard that at all times at least one person is available on the floor who can speak Spanish with customers. The important thing to remember is that the activities in your operation should always meet the standards you set for your business.

A **process** is a series of operations (tasks) that bring about a result. For example, the staffing system in your operation may include these processes:

■ Hiring

■ Training

■ Evaluating

Exhibit 1d

High-Quality Customer Service System

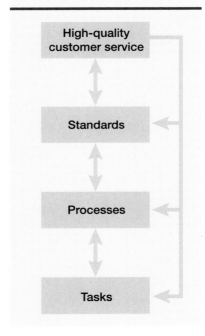

The system consists of standards, processes, and tasks organized to achieve a result; in this case, high-quality customer service.

In a customer service system, some processes include:

- Determining customers' expectations
- Satisfying customers' expectations
- Influencing customers' perceived value of service and products

Processes are composed of tasks. A **task** is a responsibility, function, or procedure that is performed as part of a process. For example, tasks that support the hiring process include:

- Writing an open position announcement
- Collecting completed applications
- Interviewing candidates

Likewise, each of the customer service processes consists of tasks. For example, the process of determining customers' needs includes these tasks:

- Asking customers what their needs are for the current visit
- Surveying customer satisfaction during or after the meal
- Offering customers an incentive for their next visit, based on the results of your questions or survey

In the following chapters, you will learn about the processes and tasks that make up a high-quality customer service system, how to design and implement such a system, and how these and other processes are used to create loyal customers and, ultimately, profit for the operation.

Impact of Customer Service

Can a business survive and be profitable while providing poor customer service? Sometimes a business has a unique product, is in a market with little or no competition, or just happens to be in the right place at the right time. Such a business can get away with providing a lower level of customer service. However, in a competitive business environment, the competition will quickly offer better service alternatives to consumers.

The quality of customer service strongly impacts a customer's dining experience. High-quality customer service leads to customer satisfaction and a good dining experience. It also adds to already good food, décor, and value, making the overall experience positive.

When thinking of an exceptional dining experience, what influences you more: service or hospitality? Why?

A few poor customer service experiences can cancel out any good impressions of food, décor, and other values, and can quickly turn the overall experience into a negative one. When customers have other dining choices, what happens if they are dissatisfied with service?

- Customer loyalty and repeat business decreases.
- Additional marketing is needed to maintain a profitable business.
- It can be difficult for the business to change its image and reputation.
- Top-quality employees may leave for better places of employment.
- Profits can decline.

Exhibit 1e

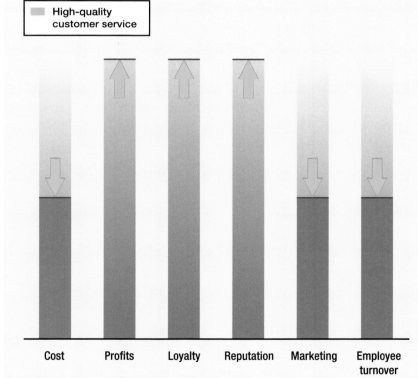

Impact of High-Quality Customer Service

Factors That Impact the Operation

However, high-quality customer service can positively impact the establishment with the following benefits (see *Exhibit 1e*):

- Leads to repeat business
- Distinguishes the establishment from its competition
- Causes customers to make a personal connection to the establishment
- Contributes to increased check and tip amounts, thereby increasing profits
- Supports marketing efforts
- Enhances the establishment's overall image and reputation
- Provides increased interaction with customers so staff can determine their needs and satisfaction
- Contributes to employee pride and satisfaction

Effect on Customer Loyalty

One impact of customer service is its effect on customer loyalty. **Customer loyalty** means that customers prefer your restaurant to all similar restaurants.

Some restaurant managers think that customer loyalty means that your restaurant is the only restaurant where the customer will dine. This is not realistic since most people do *not* eat at the same restaurant every time. There are many legitimate reasons your customers will visit many restaurants, such as:

- They want different types of service.
- They want different types of food.
- They want to experience variety.
- They are traveling in that direction.

Nevertheless, when your establishment offers what they want, your loyal customers will make your establishment their first choice.

For example, if you operate a seafood restaurant, your customers have certain expectations of your operation. If you successfully identify and consistently satisfy those expectations, the customers will identify *your* seafood restaurant as the seafood restaurant of their choice. If a customer consistently chooses your restaurant, he or she has become one of your loyal customers.

How well you identify and satisfy customer expectations will influence customer loyalty. Customer satisfaction begins with knowing customer expectations and then satisfying them. Identifying customer expectations can be challenging since each customer is different. How you can identify customer expectations is discussed later in this guide.

Effect on Marketing Success

Customers expect and accept different levels of service between a quick-service restaurant and a full-service restaurant. However, if there is a perceived or actual difference in the service level between similar types of restaurants, it is called a competitive point of difference. A **competitive point of difference** is a perceived or actual difference between any two things that can be used to influence a customer's buying decision. You can have many competitive points of difference.

A competitive point of difference can be part of a marketing strategy to separate one operation from its competition. The customer service you provide can be a competitive point of difference in your business marketing strategy. If your marketing strategy emphasizes speed (as in quick-service establishments), then customers expect speedy customer service. If you market professional and courteous staff, then that becomes the expectation of your customers. If your marketing strategy creates customer service expectations, then you must deliver them.

Effect on Reputation and Image of the Business

Another impact of customer service is its effect on business reputation or image. Word of mouth is one of the most effective forms of advertising for your business. It can enhance your reputation and image, or it can hurt it. It is not difficult to get people to talk about your business. The benefit of a good word-of-mouth reputation is that it promotes your business at no additional marketing cost to you. The challenge is to make sure that customers say positive things about your business. For example, you want customers to say things such as:

■ "You want great seafood? Go to Frenchy's Seafood on Williamson Street."

■ "Jordan's over by the stadium has the best service in town."

You want to avoid customers saying things such as:

■ "Are you sure you want to eat at The College Grill? I had a terrible experience the last time I was there."

■ "I am never going back to that bistro; the waiters are so arrogant."

Effect on Employee Turnover

Employee turnover in the restaurant and foodservice industry has been reported to be anywhere from 25 to 250 percent or higher. It is a serious issue in the industry. Reasons for this turnover include poor training, personality conflicts, poor management, moving out of town, etc.

However, another reason for employee turnover is poor customer service. The environment in which a person works has a lot to do with that person's job satisfaction. Employees who have the ability and desire to provide exceptional customer service want to work in pleasant environments. Such environments have minimal levels of complaints, chaos, uneasiness, ambiguity, stress, and lack of focus. These employees are likely to stay at their jobs. (See *Exhibit 1f*.)

Exhibit 1f

Employee satisfaction can help reduce turnover.

Effect on Profits

Customer service can also affect an operation's profits. Recall that revenue does not equal profit. There are many restaurants that generate high revenue but are not profitable. In this situation, some operations cut services to increase profits. In the short run, less training, fewer staff members, and taking shortcuts can reduce costs and increase profits. However, those cuts will result in poor service and customers will perceive less value for their dollar; eventually, they will want to go somewhere else.

However, improving your customer service can increase profits. You can do this by both taking a personal interest in your customers and suggestive selling.

Suggestive selling involves recommending additional or different items to a customer. For example, you could ask a customer, "Would you like a pastry with your coffee?" Suggestive selling can actually be a way of providing high-quality customer service. Suggestive selling should be approached as enhancing the guest experience and not as a way of increasing the check or tip. If done correctly, suggesting a side dish that will enhance an entrée, a wine that complements the main course, or a dessert to finish the evening will influence the guest's perception of value. If a suggestion results in a higher tip, a higher average check, or more profit, all the better. Suggestive selling is discussed in detail later in this guide.

Effect on Costs

Achieving high-quality customer service has an effect on costs. You can calculate or estimate a **cost-benefit ratio,** which is the dollar value of benefits divided by the dollar value of the costs necessary to achieve those benefits. You must analyze the cost-benefit ratio for high-quality customer service in order to make solid business decisions.

When restaurants do a great job at giving their guests positive experiences, the guests share their experiences and recommendations with others. As a result, the restaurant gains new customers by word of mouth rather than by spending money for marketing. The story in *Exhibit 1g* is an example of this.

In the story of Alex's birthday dinner, what did it cost the restaurant to provide that magical moment for Alex? There were costs in hiring the right person, training costs, costs in creating the culture where the servers felt empowered, and the labor costs of having those servers on duty. Now balance those costs with the benefits and the potential revenue that the experience may generate. What would it cost the restaurant to successfully influence Alex's family, friends,

Exhibit 1g

Alex's Birthday Dinner

A family of four went to a local restaurant to celebrate their four-year-old son Alex's birthday. Alex's father spoke to the host privately and asked for a slice of cake with candles for Alex's dessert. The host pleasantly and enthusiastically replied, "We would love to do this for your son. We like birthdays here. What is your son's name, and how old is he?"

Alex and his family ordered, received, and ate their meals. Everyone enjoyed the food and ambience. Then it was time for dessert. Without being told to, several servers brought out Alex's birthday cake with four candles on top. They all sang "Happy Birthday" and clapped their hands. They presented the cake to Alex and everyone could see that the icing said, "Happy Birthday Alex." The server asked Alex how old he was. When he told them, the server said, "You are so-o-o big now. I'll bet you can ride a two-wheeler," and held a short conversation with Alex. Everyone could see that Alex was happy and proud.

Then the server gave him a little package wrapped in birthday paper and tied with a bow. When Alex opened it, he was delighted to see a small toy truck. Alex squealed with delight and grinned from ear to ear. It was a magical moment for Alex.

relatives, neighbors, the people who observed that experience, and the people those witnesses told about it?

You must determine what you are willing to invest in high-quality customer service to ensure that your business consistently exceeds customers' expectations.

Making a Positive Impression

There are many benefits to creating a positive first impression. First impressions set the tone and influence customers' expectations of their experience. The benefits of a positive first impression are:

- Helps make the customer a potential return customer

- Makes customers more likely to forgive minor errors

- Serves as the least expensive and often most effective form of advertising

- Helps increase profitability

When do you think that first impression is made? Is it when customers are greeted or when they drive into the parking lot? What about the last impression; how important is that? Each opportunity to make a good or poor impression is a moment of truth.

Think About It...

"You never get a second chance to make a first impression" is a statement most people would agree with. Is the first impression truly the most important?

Moments of Truth

Karl Albrecht, in his book, *At America's Service*, defines a **moment of truth** as *"any episode in which the customer comes into contact with any aspect of the organization and gets an impression of the quality of its service."*[1]

Whenever a customer has an opportunity to form an opinion about something, it is a moment of truth. When a potential customer sees a billboard promoting a business, reads a yellow-page ad, hears from a friend about a business, drives into the parking lot, is greeted at the front door, observes spots on the silverware, or feels too hot or too cold in the dining room—are all moments of truth. There can be hundreds of moments of truth in a customer's dining experience.

Creating positive moments of truth has the following benefits:

■ Contributes to customer loyalty

■ Helps customers be more forgiving of minor mistakes

■ Provides an opportunity for positive word-of-mouth advertising

■ Allows customers to feel comfortable providing feedback

A Positive Experience

Leaving customers with a positive impression gives them a positive dining experience. But everyone has a different idea of what makes a positive experience. As discussed earlier, there are many things that influence individual expectations. However, there are some common expectations that most people have of high-quality customer service, including:

■ Use of proper telephone etiquette

■ Cleanliness of the facility both inside and outside

■ A genuine feeling of being welcome

■ Being treated with courtesy, respect, and dignity

■ Professionalism of the staff (appearance, attitude, knowledge, etc.)

Most organizations have definite policies and practices in place for all of these customer service expectations and they are included in initial training. For example, developing a feeling of being welcome and respected includes:

■ Greeting customers immediately

■ Learning customers' names and greeting them by name, if possible

■ Smiling, making eye contact, talking to, thanking, and welcoming customers

---

[1]   Albrecht, Karl. *At America's Service: How Corporations Can Revolutionize the Way They Treat Their Customers.* Homewood, IL: Dow Jones-Irwin, 1988.

Think About It...

When thinking of a dining experience, what moments of truth have you experienced?

The impression of the facility's cleanliness is also very important. You must maintain exterior facilities, such as the parking area, sidewalk, and entranceway, so that they look inviting. At a minimum, they should be free of clutter and debris. You must maintain interior facilities so they look and smell clean and fresh. This includes tables, menus, counters, and well-stocked restrooms.

However, it is difficult to train employees in how to show sincerity, helpfulness, kindness, and other behaviors. You should look for these qualities when hiring customer-contact employees. Putting the right people in the right place with the right training and tools is your responsibility.

Organizations are not perfect, and sometimes mistakes happen. However, one of your objectives in creating a positive customer impression is to ensure that there are more positive moments of truth than negative ones. Another consideration is the importance of the event in the customer's mind. For some customers, being greeted properly at the door may have less impact than being addressed properly and promptly by the server. So creating the maximum number of positive moments of truth is critical to leaving a positive impression in the customer's mind.

Exhibit 1h

Cycle of Service

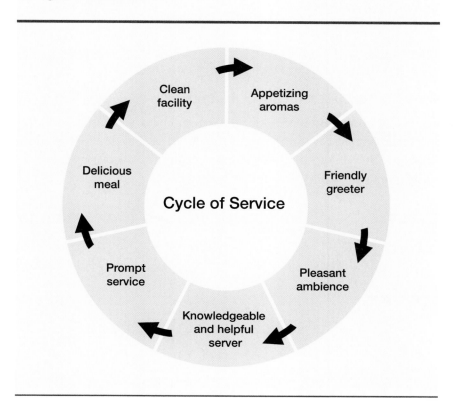

A **cycle of service** is the accumulation of all the moments of truth for a guest from beginning to end of a dining visit. (See *Exhibit 1h.*)

To get a better idea of the cycle of service, imagine you are a customer about to enter and eat at a restaurant. You will probably have moments of truth from any of the following:

- Appearance and attractiveness of the exterior
- Appetizing aromas
- Friendly greeter
- Pleasant ambience
- Knowledgeable and helpful servers
- Prompt service
- Delicious meal

The challenge faced by any business is to know when the cycle of service begins and when it ends. The cycle of service may begin when a potential customer drives by your restaurant earlier in the day and sees a littered or clean parking lot. Keep in mind that opportunities to make a judgment continue even after a customer walks out the door. If the customer had a positive cycle of service, and later praises the meal, the service, and the hospitality, you have not only taken the first step in creating a loyal customer, but that customer has also become a supporter of your establishment.

Completing the Cycle

To successfully complete the cycle of service, you must ensure that guests have as many positive moments of truth as possible. Exceeding your customers' expectations is so important to the success of your operation that you cannot leave it to chance. To determine how well your restaurant or foodservice operation meets customers' expectations, you must measure their satisfaction. Only by doing this will you know the quality of your operation's customer service, and have an idea of whether or not you are providing positive moments of truth.

There are several ways to determine customer satisfaction:

- Routinely ask whether the food, drink, service, and accommodations (seating, temperature, lighting, etc.) are satisfactory.

- Assess their satisfaction through anonymous surveys.

- Hold focus groups to get detailed feedback.

These and other customer feedback tasks will be covered in more detail in a later chapter. For now, you must understand that developing and implementing methods for determining customer satisfaction is a measure of the quality of your customer service.

Activity

Analysis of Actual Customer Service Observation

Observe a dining experience for yourself or someone else. You may observe any dining establishment—high-quality customer service is not limited to full-service or fine-dining establishments. However, remember that customer service expectations are influenced by the type of establishment. Complete the form below. Know the content of the form well enough so you can make observations without the staff's awareness. After you have completed the observation, write a brief analysis of what you have learned. You can discuss product knowledge, communication skills, employees' attitudes, employees' appearances, and how your expectations and decision-making were influenced.

Rate the following on a scale from 1-5:

1 = Not acceptable   4 = Exceeds expectation
2 = Below expectation   5 = Outstanding
3 = Meets expectation

Please include comments if you give a rating of "1" or "5" on this form. Comments for other scores are also helpful. You may add questions or points of observation to this list.

1 Overall appearance of the facility from the outside   ① ② ③ ④ ⑤
Comments:

2 Greeting by the staff   ① ② ③ ④ ⑤
Comments:

3 Overall appearance of the facility from the inside   ① ② ③ ④ ⑤
Comments:

4 Appearance of the staff   ① ② ③ ④ ⑤
Comments:

5 Cleanliness of the facility   ① ② ③ ④ ⑤
Comments:

6 Professionalism of the staff   ① ② ③ ④ ⑤
Comments:

continued on next page

Analysis of Actual Customer Service Observation *continued from previous page*

7 Product knowledge of the staff
Comments:
① ② ③ ④ ⑤

8 Quality of the service
Comments:
① ② ③ ④ ⑤

9 Promptness of the staff
Comments:
① ② ③ ④ ⑤

10 Professional appearance
Comments:
① ② ③ ④ ⑤

11 Management visibility
Comments:
① ② ③ ④ ⑤

12 Adequate staffing
Comments:
① ② ③ ④ ⑤

13 Staff pleasantness
Comments:
① ② ③ ④ ⑤

14 Problems solved effectively
Comments:
① ② ③ ④ ⑤

15 Your experience made you feel like a valued customer
Comments:
① ② ③ ④ ⑤

16 Overall evaluation of customer service
Comments:
① ② ③ ④ ⑤

Summary

Customer service impacts all aspects of business, such as revenue, profit, cost, the guest, and the employee. High-quality customer service consists of service and hospitality, which includes the products provided and the feeling customers take with them. Influencing the customer's perception of value and consistently meeting or exceeding customer expectations leads to customer loyalty and profit. The best way to accomplish this is to implement and manage a high-quality customer service system that ensures your marketing promises are fulfilled. The restaurant and foodservice industry is extremely competitive. High-quality customer service can be the competitive edge that allows a business to set the standard and become the benchmark for the competition. Creating positive impressions, moments of truth, and an overall positive cycle of service will help you achieve the many benefits of high-quality customer service. Customer service can impact many areas of the operation such as loyalty, marketing, reputation, turnover, costs, and profits.

Review Your Learning

1 A high-quality customer service system is supported by

A. repeat customers.

B. glamorous décor.

C. processes and tasks.

D. first impressions.

2 Customer loyalty is

A. easy to achieve only if the product satisfies the customer.

B. a result of management interaction with the customer.

C. not necessary if your business has a competitive point of difference.

D. achieved by providing the product and service the customer expects.

3 Restaurant managers believe that good customer service is important to their operations because it can

A. increase management salaries.

B. decrease marketing expenditures.

C. improve kitchen efficiency.

D. decrease the cost of labor.

4 A competitive point of difference is the

A. actual difference between any two things done by competitors that influence customers.

B. perceived difference between any two things done by competitors.

C. actual or perceived difference between any two things that influence customers.

D. hidden difference between any two or more things done by competitors.

5 All of the following are competitive points of difference for an operation *except* the

A. level of service provided to the guest.

B. skills and experience level of the staff.

C. variety of menu offerings.

D. financial strength of the operation.

6 The impact of customer service affects which aspects of a restaurant?

A. Revenue, food cost, and profit

B. Staffing, training, and supplier selection

C. Profit, interest rates, and dividends

D. Marketing, staffing, and profit

7 Higher levels of customer service result in

A. lower profits for the restaurant.

B. increased customer loyalty.

C. higher turnover for the restaurant.

D. increased costs and expenses.

8 The cycle of service is

A. all the expectations from the beginning to the end of a meal.

B. all the steps in providing good customer service, from designing the menu to serving the food and drinks.

C. all the customer's moments of truth from the beginning to the end of a visit.

D. all the interactions a guest receives from service providers during a single visit to a restaurant or foodservice operation.

9 A "moment of truth" is

A. any opportunity a person has to make a judgment about service quality.

B. the first impression a person has of a restaurant or foodservice operation.

C. the last impression a person has of a restaurant or foodservice operation.

D. the accumulation of all the customer service a guest encounters.

10 Anupa's favorite sushi restaurant offers a hot towel at the beginning of the meal, and the server always pleasantly says, "We are very pleased to have you with us this evening." This is an example of

A. customer satisfaction.

B. hospitality.

C. suggestive selling.

D. cycle of service.

Notes

Basic Concepts for High-Quality Customer Service

After completing this chapter, you should be able to:

- Define and distinguish between internal and external customers.
- Explain the high-quality customer service system.
- Describe the systems management approach.
- Describe the service-profit chain.
- Explain how the service-profit chain relates to the high-quality customer service system.

Test Your Knowledge

1 **True or False:** The customer you should satisfy in an operation is the guest. *(See p. 25.)*

2 **True or False:** Systems management is an old concept in the restaurant and foodservice industry. *(See p. 28.)*

3 **True or False:** The service-profit chain describes how profit and lower food costs are linked in a high-quality customer service system. *(See p. 30.)*

4 **True or False:** An important part of a high-quality customer-service system is profit. *(See p. 27.)*

5 **True or False:** The service-profit chain focuses mainly on internal customers. *(See p. 30.)*

Key Terms

Customer

External customer

Input-output relationship

Internal customer

Service-profit chain

Systems management approach

Exhibit 2a

Good customer service can be a competitive point of difference.

Introduction

In every category of foodservice—price, menu, or style of service—there are many establishments a guest can choose from when deciding where to dine. For many customers, receiving the high-quality customer service appropriate for the type of establishment they choose can be the competitive point of difference for a restaurant operator. (See *Exhibit 2a.*)

Also, restaurant and foodservice operations are becoming so complex and profit margins so tight that a successful manager must be good at many things. You must be able to see the "big picture" as well as the little details in how things in the operation relate to and impact each other. You must then be able to make adjustments based on these relationships and their impact. A systems approach to managing enables you to make complex business-sensitive responses to business conditions that involve the nature and quality of customer service. This is essential because the profitability of the operation depends on your success or failure to make correct decisions and provide high-quality customer service.

In order to understand these relationships and their impact on customer service, this chapter will take a look at:

■ The customer

■ High-quality customer service

■ A high-quality customer service system

■ Systems management and how it applies to the restaurant industry

■ How the service-profit chain deals with the difficulties of providing high-quality customer service, while maintaining a profitable business

Who Is the Customer?

Recall that a moment of truth is any episode in which the customer comes into contact with any aspect of the organization and gets an impression of the quality of its service. A critical part of this definition is the customer. But who is the customer here? Many people would identify the guest as the customer. That is correct; however, Joseph Juran, a noted expert on quality, presents a more complex description of a customer. To paraphrase Juran, a **customer** is anyone who is influenced by or has influence on a product, service, system, or process.[1]

In Juran's view, there are external customers and internal customers. (See *Exhibit 2b*.) An **external customer** is the end receiver of a product or service and is outside the boundaries of an organization. In a restaurant, the guest is the external customer. An **internal customer** is anyone inside an organization who receives products, services, or information from someone else to complete his or her work. The restaurant's employees (and even its suppliers) are internal

Exhibit 2b

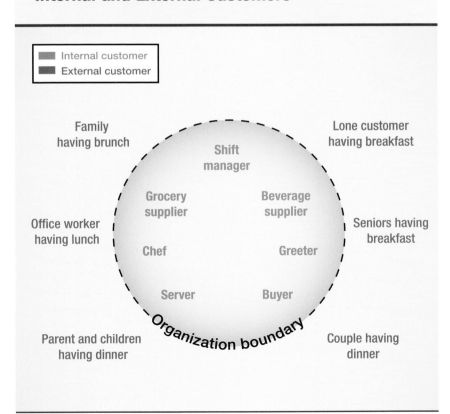

Internal and External Customers

■ Internal customer
■ External customer

Family having brunch

Shift manager

Lone customer having breakfast

Grocery supplier

Beverage supplier

Office worker having lunch

Seniors having breakfast

Chef

Greeter

Server

Buyer

Parent and children having dinner

Organization boundary

Couple having dinner

[1] Juran, Joseph, A. Blanton Godfrey. *Juran's Quality Handbook,* 5th Edition. McGraw Hill, 1998.

Think About It...

What other customer relationships exist in a restaurant or foodservice establishment?

customers and affect the products, services, systems, or processes. Like external customers, internal customers can experience moments of truth in every interaction they have with external customers, other employees, and management. Satisfying both internal and external customers is critical to providing high-quality customer service.

Another way to think of the customer is as someone on the receiving end of any input-output relationship. An **input-output relationship** is any interaction between two people or two groups where the work product of one is used by the other. An example of this is the typical sequence of service in a restaurant. (See *Exhibit 2c*.)

Exhibit 2c

Primary Restaurant and Foodservice Customer Relationship

Internal customer
External customer

1 Places dinner order   **2 Places dinner order**

Guest   Server   Chef

4 Delivers dinner order   **3 Delivers dinner order**

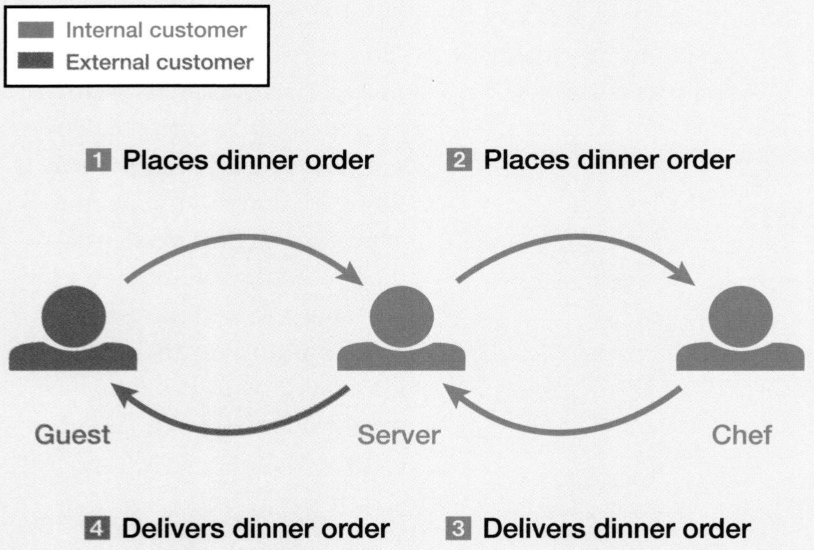

1 The guest, the external customer, provides input to the server by making a request, such as ordering a menu item. The server receives this request (information) and becomes an internal customer of the guest.

2 The server gives the request (provides input) to the chef. The chef receives the order and becomes an internal customer of the server.

3 The chef prepares and gives the ordered food (provides output) to the server. The server receives the ordered food and becomes an internal customer of the chef.

4 The server delivers the ordered food (provides output) to the guest. The guest receives the ordered food and is the external customer of the restaurant.

With this definition of a customer as someone on the receiving end of an input-output relationship, you can see how both internal and external customers are equally important when providing high-quality customer service.

Activity

Analysis of Typical Customer Interactions

On a separate sheet of paper answer the following six questions for each interaction listed below.

1. What is the input/output relationship?

2. Who is the internal customer? Who is the external customer?

3. What are the possible moments of truth associated with this interaction?

4. What would make these positive or negative moments of truth?

5. Who determines whether the relationship is positive or negative?

6. Who controls the situation?

Interaction 1: A greeter meets guests at the door and welcomes them to the restaurant.

Interaction 2: A sommelier presents the wine list to a guest and says that she would be happy to make suggestions.

Interaction 3: A line cook asks a server to clarify an order.

Interaction 4: A manager walks around the dining room asking guests about their dining experience.

Interaction 5: A manager places a special request order with a produce vendor.

High-Quality Customer Service

One of the objectives of every business should be to satisfy the customer by providing high-quality customer service. There is a lot more to customer satisfaction than the temperature of the food and the environment in which the food is served. High-quality customer service means consistently exceeding customer expectations for products and the nature of services received, and for personal interaction during the delivery, to create value for the customer and profit for the organization.

High-quality customer service can be divided into four parts, which are addressed in later chapters:

- Identifying customer expectations (Chapter 3)

- Consistently exceeding customer expectations (Chapter 4)

- Providing products and services that create value for the customer (Chapter 4)

- Creating profit for the organization (Chapter 5)

Exhibit 2d

Achieving High-Quality Customer Service

Create profits

Identify customer expectations

Design, implement and manage a system to:

Provide products and services

Exceed customer expectations

Design, implement, and manage a system for the four parts of high-quality customer service.

These four parts of high-quality customer service cannot be achieved automatically or easily. To successfully provide quality customer service, you must develop, implement, and manage a high-quality customer service system that addresses all four parts. (See *Exhibit 2d*.) In the restaurant and foodservice industry, this is most effectively done by using a systems management approach.

Systems Management Approach

Systems management as a way to handle work is a relatively new concept in the restaurant and foodservice industry. A systems management approach looks at the activities in your operation as a group of different processes and tasks that work together to meet both the objectives of each process and of the whole operation.

Operations use many different processes every day. Each process consists of specific tasks that are done to your standards so that you can achieve the results you want. Examples of specific processes in a restaurant include:

- Dining room functions
- Reservation management
- Purchasing
- Food preparation

The tasks that make up processes are usually the activities completed by your staff members. For example, a typical task in a reservation management process is to record a reservation. Properly performing tasks will help meet the goals of each individual process.

To effectively manage the high-quality customer service system, you must understand

- how it works.

- the ways processes depend on each other.

- how each task contributes to a process.

- the expectations of external customers.

- what happens if external customers are dissatisfied and do not perceive value in the dining experience.

- internal customer needs or the result may be loss of productivity or employee turnover.

- all the steps in your processes.

This is just as important as understanding how the whole system works. Make sure all steps are completed properly or quality will suffer. Since the goal of a high-quality customer service system is to consistently exceed customer expectations, the processes in a high-quality customer service system must also include the four parts of high-quality customer service.

A key characteristic of systems management is that processes affect each other. You should have cross-functional knowledge and experience either from your own operational background or from management training. In other words, you must know about the different processes and tasks in the operation and how they work. You must also understand how all the processes and their tasks depend on each other. For example, if a server gives the wrong order to the kitchen, the wrong entrée is prepared, and the guest experiences a negative moment of truth when the server delivers the wrong meal. In another example, when bussing is properly done, the dining room is clean, seating is available, and the dishes are put in the dishwasher to be cleaned and reused.

You also must be able to recognize cross-functional issues to correct problems at the source. Many problems can be traced to a breakdown in the system instead of the staff's expertise. For example, an unusually long service time may be the result of an item being understocked at the cook's station, not because of the cook's skills.

Exhibit 2e

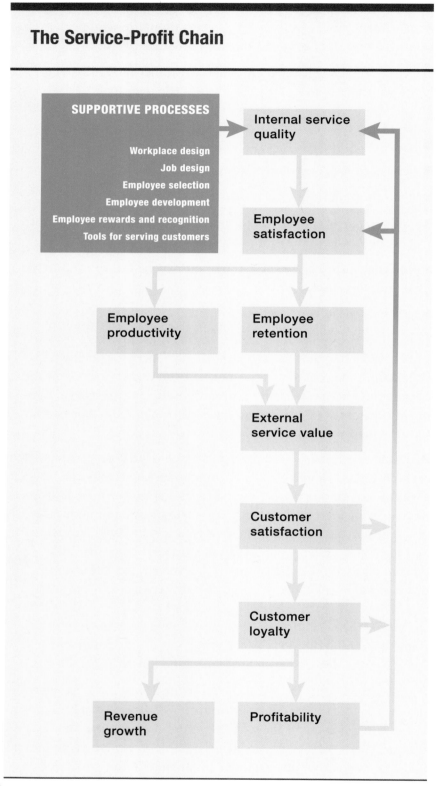

The Service-Profit Chain

SUPPORTIVE PROCESSES

Workplace design
Job design
Employee selection
Employee development
Employee rewards and recognition
Tools for serving customers

Internal service quality

Employee satisfaction

Employee productivity

Employee retention

External service value

Customer satisfaction

Customer loyalty

Revenue growth

Profitability

Adapted from: Hasket, James L., Thomas O. Jones, Gary W. Loveman, W. Earl Sasser, Jr., and Leonard A. Schlesinger. *"Putting the Service-Profit Chain to Work."* Harvard Business Review. March–April 1994, p.166.

From a systems management view, the operation can perform well only when all the systems function properly.

The Service-Profit Chain

The **service-profit chain** in *Exhibit 2e* shows how profit and revenue growth are linked in a high-quality customer service system. The service-profit chain shows that when a business successfully satisfies internal and external customers, costs are reduced and productivity is increased. This exhibit also shows some of the processes that support the high-quality customer service system.

Supportive Processes

Exhibit 2e also shows the supportive processes in the operation. Supportive processes are the elements in your establishment that impact your internal customers (employees) to help them perform their jobs and be satisfied. These elements include:

■ **Workplace design**—Environmental conditions, safety issues, traffic flow, employee spaces such as locker rooms, restrooms, and break rooms—plus the look and feel of these behind-the-scene areas

Exhibit 2f

Supportive processes such as good job design allow employees to perform their tasks more effectively.

- **Job design**—Job processes, work allocation, tools and equipment, job descriptions, job analysis, and team design (see *Exhibit 2f*)

- **Employee selection and Employee development**—Policies and practices for recruitment, hiring, placement, training, and retention

- **Employee rewards and recognition**—Wages, benefits, incentive programs, personal recognition such as monthly birthday parties, reward certificates, contests, and managerial practices

- **Tools for serving customers**—Uniforms, properly maintained equipment, cross-training, service skills training, and processes to determine customer expectations and evaluate customer service

The supportive processes directly affect the internal service quality component in the service-profit chain. Internal service quality is the degree to which you provide the various workplace elements to keep internal customers satisfied. Higher-quality supportive processes lead to high-quality internal service quality, which increases employee satisfaction.

The following are descriptions of each component in the service-profit chain.

- **Internal service quality**—Employees are happy in their jobs when the workplace is pleasant to work in, they have the right tools, their skills and careers are developed, and they receive good rewards and recognition.

■ **Employee satisfaction**—Good internal customer service, as provided by the supportive processes, leads to satisfied employees. They spend little time complaining, develop greater skills, stay on the job longer, and are able to do their jobs better.

■ **Employee retention**—A satisfied employee is more productive and stays on the job longer, turning it into a career. A satisfied employee will not look for better work environments or better wages and benefits. Satisfied employees are effective workers who stay and do not have to be replaced. This eliminates the costs of locating, hiring, and training new employees.

■ **Employee productivity**—Productive, long-term employees provide a higher level of service at a reduced cost over time. This is because they have higher skills and interest levels than unsatisfied employees. Also, the training that you give them will return benefits for their entire time with you.

These four components make up the employee satisfaction portion of the chain. As a manager, you can greatly influence and control these components in your operation. The following components show how satisfied employees tend to provide better service for guests. The guests then perceive more value and satisfaction in your products and services, which will eventually translate into higher profitability for your operation.

■ **External service value**—The higher level of service provided by productive, long-term employees has greater value for external customers. These employees have greater expertise in helping customers select food and beverage items and will provide a good dining experience because they are good at service and personal interaction. This dining experience gives guests more pleasure and better dollar value.

■ **Customer satisfaction**—Customers who receive better service are more satisfied. They feel more appreciated, and like the higher-quality service they receive. They also feel they are getting more for their money.

■ **Customer loyalty**—Satisfied customers are more loyal. They return often to the establishment, tell others or bring them, and increase the establishment's customer base.

■ **Revenue growth**—Getting more customers means increased overall revenue.

■ **Profitability**—Profitability results when the components in the service-profit chain are achieved in a cost-effective way. For example, when customer loyalty increases, some expenses, such as advertising and marketing, should decrease.

The service-profit chain contains an important feedback loop that takes the information and money from the customer satisfaction, customer loyalty, profitability, and revenue growth components and uses them to improve the internal service quality and employee satisfaction components. In a good service-profit chain, some of the revenue growth is also put back or looped into the high-quality customer service system to continuously improve it. Chapters 3 through 5 discuss the various aspects of the service-profit chain in more detail.

Having satisfied employees is so important to the success of an operation that the National Restaurant Association Educational Foundation and Coca-Cola have established the prestigious Spirit Awards program. These annual awards honor those operators who truly understand that enhancing employee satisfaction ultimately leads to guest satisfaction.

Having satisfied employees is only part of the process of creating satisfied external customers over a long period of time. The external customers make the business succeed or fail.

Activity

How Is Quality Determined in the Restaurant and Foodservice Industry?

Brainstorm a list of how quality in the restaurant and foodservice industry is determined. Discuss how guest perception of a high-quality customer service system has changed over the last twenty-five years. Topics may include, but are not limited to, menu, service style, variety, competition, and how the industry responds to the demand for increased quality.

Summary

In today's competitive market, the successful owner or manager in the restaurant and foodservice industry needs to attract and retain customers, both internal (employees) and external (guests). Customers are involved in an input-output relationship with each other all the time. Satisfying internal customers greatly improves the chances of satisfying external customers. Developing, implementing, and managing a system that enables you to provide high-quality customer service by understanding how different aspects of the operation affect each other is one of the keys to a successful career in the restaurant and foodservice industry. Understanding the service-profit chain and taking a systems management approach to high-quality customer service is the most effective and efficient way to satisfy internal and external customers and be profitable over time.

Review Your Learning

1 All of the following are part of high-quality customer service *except*

A. identifying customer expectations.

B. using cost-cutting approaches.

C. meeting expectations.

D. generating profit.

2 A customer is

A. any guest of the operation.

B. influenced by a product or service.

C. the one who actually pays the bill.

D. everyone at one time or another in the service-profit chain.

3 A high-quality customer service system considers

A. only the expectations of the manager.

B. the expectations and needs of the system.

C. both the internal and external customer.

D. work standards provided by management.

4 In a systems management approach,

A. your concern should be the process that loses money.

B. you must be aware of cross-functional issues.

C. you do not have to provide services.

D. the processes only work independently of each other.

5 A high-quality customer service system can lead to which of the following?

A. The loss of employees

B. The loss of external customers

C. Customer satisfaction

D. Profit reduction

6 The result of the service-profit chain is

A. a systems approach to management.

B. revenue growth and profit.

C. profit only.

D. reinvestment of losses.

7 According to the service-profit chain, all of the following increase customer satisfaction *except*

A. treating employees as external customers.

B. employee development programs.

C. employee rewards and recognition programs.

D. employee productivity improvements.

8 The loop aspect of the service-profit chain refers to

A. reinvesting in a high-quality service system.

B. the feedback from competitive establishments.

C. using profits to diversify the owner's investments.

D. the fact that revenue growth always results in profit growth.

9 To ensure the best chance to provide high-quality customer service,

A. the external customer must come first.

B. the internal and external customer must be valued equally.

C. the internal customer must come first.

D. the business must be profitable above anything else.

Identifying Customer Expectations

3

Inside This Chapter
- Identifying Internal Customer Expectations
- Identifying External Customer Expectations
- Obtaining Feedback from Internal and External Customers

After completing this chapter, you should be able to:
- Identify ways to staff properly to ensure prompt, friendly, and courteous customer service.
- Explain the importance of determining customers' expectations.
- Describe internal and external customer expectations.
- List the tools and methods for identifying customer expectations and feedback.
- Explain the importance of gathering feedback from customers.
- List the types of feedback to be obtained from internal and external customers.

Test Your Knowledge

1. **True or False:** Employee development, job design, and tools and equipment are some employee concerns. *(See p. 37.)*

2. **True or False:** Guest expectations are more important than employee expectations. *(See p. 36.)*

3. **True or False:** Treat right is one of the four rights for achieving internal service quality. *(See p. 38.)*

4. **True or False:** Determining customer expectations can be a simple process or a complex one, depending on your operation. *(See p. 43.)*

5. **True or False:** Observations by waitstaff are an important source of data on guest satisfaction. *(See p. 44.)*

Key Terms

Comment cards

Compensation

Competitive analysis

Consumer research

Demographic analysis

Focus groups

Four rights

Job design

Mystery shoppers

Objective methods

Secret shoppers

Standard deviation

Statistical analysis systems (SAS)

Surveys

Test marketing

Tools and equipment

Workplace design

Think About It...

There is a common customer expectation in the restaurant and foodservice industry for an establishment to have a clean, safe, and friendly environment. What are some less common customer expectations?

Introduction

Perceptions of high-quality customer service have evolved throughout history. Customers dining at an inn during the eighteenth century had quite different expectations from customers dining in today's restaurants. Also, today's customers have different expectations when dining at different types of foodservice establishments, such as quick-service, casual, fine-dining, etc. Identifying customer expectations is critical to achieving high-quality customer service. Once you have identified the expectations, you must satisfy them, and then confirm that they were satisfied.

Identifying Internal Customer Expectations

Chapter 2 described two types of customers: external and internal. You should identify the expectations of both of these customers in order to satisfy them.

Exhibit 3a

The Service-Profit Chain

SUPPORTIVE PROCESSES

Workplace design
Job design
Employee selection
Employee development
Employee rewards and recognition
Tools for serving customers

- Internal service quality
- Employee satisfaction
- Employee productivity
- Employee retention
- External service value
- Customer satisfaction
- Customer loyalty
- Revenue growth
- Profitability

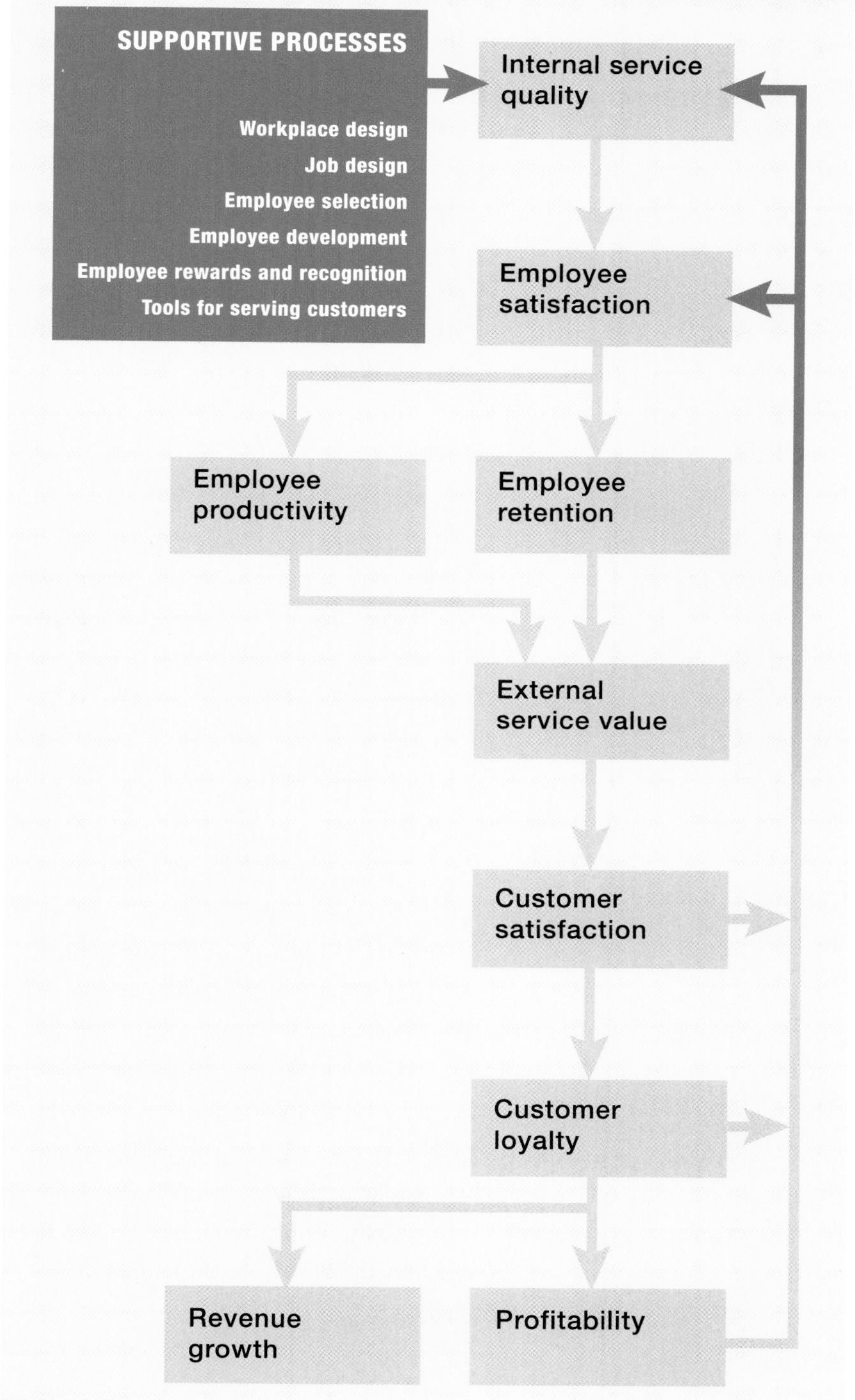

Adapted from: Hasket, James L., Thomas O. Jones, Gary W. Loveman, W. Earl Sasser, Jr., and Leonard A. Schlesinger. *"Putting the Service-Profit Chain to Work."* Harvard Business Review. March–April 1994, p.166.

A high-quality customer service system starts with an operation's internal customers. The internal service quality step from the service-profit chain (see *Exhibit 3a*) is an excellent starting point for identifying internal customer expectations. Some methods to help you satisfy and retain employees, and ensure internal service quality are:

- Hire the correct individuals.
- Provide appropriate training.
- Compensate employees properly.
- Supply enough high-quality tools and equipment.
- Recognize employees' good work.
- Correct employees' mistakes graciously.

The supportive processes of internal service quality are the major concerns of your employees:

- Workplace design
- Job design
- Employee selection
- Employee development
- Employee rewards and recognition
- Necessary tools and equipment

Successfully implementing these supportive processes will help make a satisfied internal customer.

When trying to identify internal customer expectations, you should know the factors that satisfy them. These factors are known as the four rights.

The **four rights** describe ways to hire, train, compensate, and retain employees, which will enable you to satisfy them and achieve internal service quality. (See *Exhibit 3b.*) The four rights are:

- Hire right
- Train right
- Compensate right
- Retain right

To attain these four rights, you must know your internal customer's expectations in these four areas.

Exhibit 3b

Four Rights

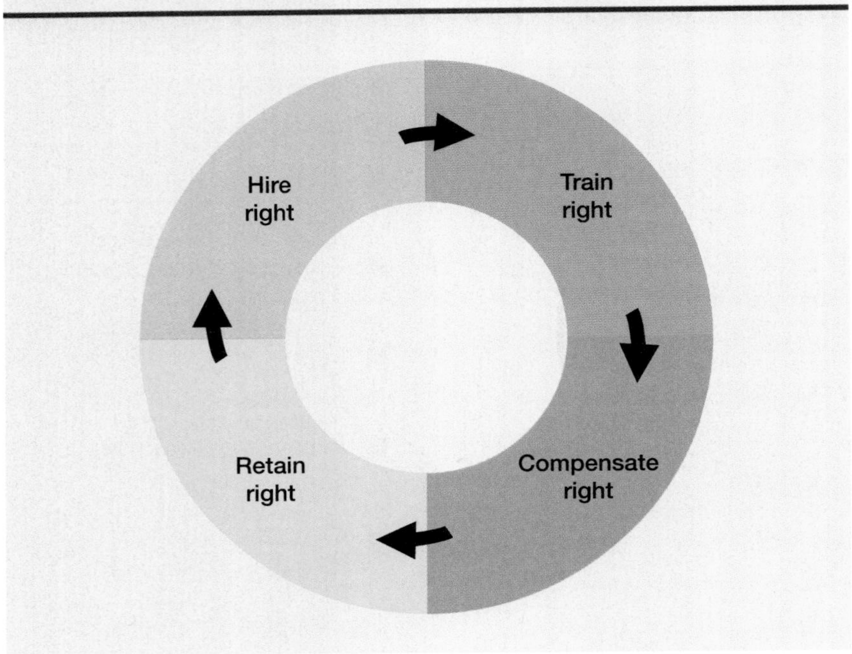

All four rights must work together to make a satisfied internal customer.

Hire Right

"Hire right" refers to the supportive process of employee selection. Staffing a restaurant is an extremely challenging task. In many markets, attracting the best employees is as competitive, if not more so, as attracting guests. However, it is important that you hire the right people for your operation. When you open a new restaurant or increase or replace staff at an existing one, the hiring pressure can be tremendous. Many managers cope with the pressure by hiring anyone that is available. This is not the best way to staff a restaurant.

To prevent long-term staffing problems, you should make the *right* hiring choice, not the *convenient* one. It is much better to have a pool of potential employees to draw from when you need to, such as to replace a current staff member who leaves. You can develop this pool in the following ways:

- Employee referrals
- Recent qualified applicants who were not hired
- Former employees who might be willing to return

Exhibit 3c

Take the time to train your employees to support their development.

Train Right

According to many industry professionals, the main reason for employee turnover is poor training. After hiring the right employees, training is the most important factor in achieving internal service quality. (See *Exhibit 3c.*) For experienced new hires, training may be as simple as identifying the differences between their previous place of employment and yours. For new hires with little or no experience, the training program must be extensive and thorough. These employees should be taught basics such as:

- Telephone etiquette
- Guest welcoming and seating protocols
- Accurately taking and recording guest orders
- Table setup
- Serving food
- Correctly managing and pacing the flow of a meal
- Food safety

Each operation should have a booklet outlining policies, procedures, and setups, and they should also be included in the new employee training program. You should give a copy of this booklet to each new employee and keep a reference copy in each workstation. Cross-training employees in a variety of jobs within the organization is a good way to keep them excited about working. It also provides you with flexibility for scheduling.

Compensate Right

When "compensating right," **compensation** refers to the various programs and practices of employee reward and recognition, including benefits, incentive programs, flexible schedules, and rewards programs. All these factors should be part of a comprehensive compensation package since compensation is not limited just to pay.

Many restaurant and foodservice operations have scholarship programs for employees. Employee benefits, such as paid vacation and health insurance, are becoming more available to both full- and part-time employees. The more benefits that an operation provides, the better employees it can acquire and the longer it can retain them.

Retain Right

Almost all of the successful operators in the industry have said, "Surround yourself with good people." Unfortunately, just hiring them right, training them right, and compensating them right is not enough. To retain good employees, you also have to adequately supply the other things that they seek:

- Good workplace design
- Good job design
- Good tools and equipment

Workplace design refers to the facility, the front of the house, and the back of the house. In some newer restaurants, kitchen floor plans are designed to maximize traffic flow and work efficiency. In some designs, for a fully staffed establishment, a worker only has to take one step to the right or the left to complete a task.

The proper tools for good workplace design include:

- Cooking utensils
- Cleaning equipment
- Bartending tools
- Effective and efficient procedures
- Verified and documented recipes
- Uniforms
- Point-of-sale (POS) and other computer systems
- Order pads
- Receipts
- Photographs of proper plate presentations
- Properly calibrated ovens, fryers, and cooling units

Job design describes the specific characteristics of a job. A well-designed job helps get the work done effectively and efficiently. It should contain a logical set of tasks that clearly lead to an end product that employees can identify as their work. This provides the employees with both a sense of worth and a meaningful contribution, and makes supervising easier. A well-designed job uses the simplest job processes to meet job requirements without complicating them. It also helps identify employees' personal needs for the following:

- Number and details of tasks

- Amount of variation in tasks

- Amount of empowerment the employee has in selecting activities and outcomes

- Number of other employees that a person works with regularly and the nature of the relationship (receiving orders, giving orders, cooperatively making decisions, receiving raw materials from, and giving finished products to)

- Frequency, nature, and source of feedback about job performance

- Amount and frequency of compensation from hourly pay to job perks and bonuses

By having jobs that are well designed, everyone wins. Employees have a pleasant and meaningful work experience, and the operation gets the work done in the most effective and efficient manner.

Tools and equipment are essential resources needed for employees to effectively do the job. When employees have proper tools and other resources that they need, they are more efficient and less frustrated. This will benefit the operation, satisfy internal customers, and help provide high-quality customer service to everyone.

If you take the concept of "retain right" just a little further, it can also help identify employees that are not a good fit for the operation to help ensure you have employees who *are* a good fit.

Identifying Employee Expectations

Finding out the unique expectations of internal customers is an ongoing challenge for most employers. This process should start before an employee is hired, and it should continue as long as the employee is with the operation.

During Hiring

Determining employee expectations during the interview process can be a very effective way to avoid making hiring mistakes. When you are interviewing a candidate for a position in your operation, some questions you might ask include:

- How many hours a week are you able to work?

- What other jobs have you had that you liked—what was it about them you liked?

- What were some things you did not like about your last job?

- Do you have scheduling requirements that need accommodation?

Checking with references is another way to get some indication about what a candidate may expect from an employer.

What employees expect in a job can be influenced when *you* communicate *your* expectations to them, even as early as during the hiring process. Today, many operations communicate their expectations to a potential employee before the job application is completed or during the first interview. Once the employer's expectations are clear, the candidate must decide whether he or she can meet them. Only then does the candidate decide to complete the hiring process. Organizations following this model experience a higher retention for those candidates that they eventually hire. This noticeably reduces an organization's turnover cost.

Gathering Expectations of Existing Employees

It is not enough to learn employees' expectations when they start with your operation. Gathering information about employee expectations should be a continual process that does not have to be awkward and formal. There are many easy ways to be aware of employees' needs and concerns, including:

- Monitoring different processes in the operation to see which ones appear inefficient (See *Exhibit 3d.*)

- Asking how things are going, both at one-on-one and routine meetings

- Having an employee suggestion box

- Posting a list of issues on the employee bulletin board and letting employees anonymously vote for the one that concerns them the most

- Listening carefully to employees when they ask for something

- Observing employees at work to see if anything causes them problems

Exhibit 3d

Monitoring processes and observing employees can help you identify concerns or expectations that employees have and ways to improve processes.

Identifying External Customer Expectations

Identifying external customer expectations can be simple or complex, depending on the size and information needs of your operation. A small, single-location restaurant will likely have simple needs and methods for determining external customer expectations, whereas a major chain with thousands of restaurants nationwide will probably have complex needs and methods.

The Nature of External Customer Expectations

There is an assumption that external customers have common expectations, such as wanting a clean, safe, and friendly dining environment. However, external customers may want many particular things from your establishment, such as:

- Certain type or size of table

- Specific table location

- Special diet, such as one without allergens or one that follows religious requirements

- Favorite item that is not on the menu but might be prepared

- Recognition of a special occasion, such as a birthday or anniversary

- Separate room for privacy or a meeting

- Help in ordering food or wine

- Help reading or interpreting the menu, especially for a foreign-language speaker or a person with a disability

- Certain type of music, or a change in the music volume

- Room temperature and lighting changes

- Place to smoke, or a place to avoid smoke

Employees with customer contact are responsible for uncovering these and other needs in a respectful and helpful way.

External customer expectations can be affected by where and how they fit into any or all of the following categories:

- Age group

- Relationship status: single, couple, family, group, etc.

- Size of party

- Business or casual

- Dietary needs

- First-time, occasional, or regular guest

- Special occasion

- Large groups

- Language or disability limitations needing accommodation or assistance

It is important that you establish processes to determine the needs and expectations of your external customers. You must train your employees on these processes to ensure that they are done properly and you get the information you need. The next section describes some of these processes.

Gathering Information about Expectations

There are several ways to gather information about the needs and wants of external customers:

- Employee observation and questioning

- Engaging in conversation with guests

- Simple and complex consumer research

Employee Observation and Questioning

You must have the right employees in place to effectively and respectfully gather data. Properly completing the four rights for internal customers allows your operation to put the best people in place to do an excellent job, especially at providing high-quality customer service to external customers. Important jobs with external customer contact are:

- Greeter or host

- Dining room server

- Bartender or bar server

- Dining room manager

- Establishment manager

All of these employees can observe and question customers and should have the responsibility of determining and satisfying customer expectations.

The greeter or host probably has the most responsibilities in this area. The greeter's role is to provide the best first impression in appearance, friendliness, and interest in meeting a guests' needs. To do this, the greeter should evaluate where and how guests fit in to the previously-mentioned categories, determine their specific needs for the current visit, and communicate those needs to the appropriate staff members.

During the greeting process, there are several opportunities for input and output and moments of truth for both external and internal customers.

Consider the following two scenarios. Which one provides greater customer satisfaction?

Scenario One: Greeter One says, "Good evening. How many in your party? Smoking or nonsmoking?" And then proceeds to seat the party at the next table to be filled.

Scenario Two: Greeter Two says: "Good evening, welcome to Charlie's. Did you have any trouble finding us or parking? How many are in your party? What kind of table would you like?" The greeter escorts them to such a table. "Here are today's specials to look over. Your server will be Tony; he will be right over to get you started and explain the specials."

In the above scenarios, Greeter Two shows a good example of appropriate guest questioning and service. Perhaps Greeter One needed more training or should not have been placed in the greeter position in the first place. Employees can be trained to observe and ask questions in order to determine guest categorization and expectations, but some people are just better at interacting with others in a friendly and courteous way.

Engaging in Conversation with Guests

A powerful approach for determining guests' wants and needs is to engage in light conversation with them. During the discussion, an employee can find out many things about guests, including what they want at the time and any special needs they have. (See *Exhibit 3e.*) This conversational approach can make the guest feel like a true guest, instead of simply a customer. This approach can be part of an operation's style, or it can be an individual practice. Any employee with guest contact, but especially the greeter, can converse with a guest.

There are two important points to remember when using this approach:

■ **People react poorly to phoniness.** You should ask questions and engage in conversation that is genuine. Not everyone can do this with strangers, and it is difficult to train someone to engage in conversation. If conversation is important to your operation's style, then you should seek this ability when hiring employees.

Exhibit 3e

Having genuine conversations with guests can help you find out their expectations.

■ **Not everyone wants to be your friend.** Some guests never want to engage in conversation; other guests want to converse on some visits and not on others. You should ensure that all managers and staff with customer contact can recognize cues that indicate when guests do not want conversation and prefer minimal interaction. Training can provide skills in this area.

Simple Consumer Research

Objective methods for gathering information from your customers can include simple surveys or comment cards. Comment cards are discussed later in this chapter, but the most typical objective way to determine external customer expectations is through a simple survey. A **survey** is a series of specific questions an operation asks about one or more topics such as menu, food, service, décor, etc. Surveys may be multiple choice or short answer. They may be written or conducted as interviews. Written ones may be on table cards, larger paper, or an interactive Web form. Keep in mind that even a short, easy-to-complete survey requires more preparation and more analysis than simply questioning customers and engaging in conversation with them.

Complex Consumer Research

Consumer research includes methods of investigation that are directed at discovering the products and services customers want and are willing to buy. They gather input from more consumers than your operation's existing customer base. Consumer research includes complex surveys, focus groups, test marketing, competitive analysis, and demographic analysis. These methods are used to collect more specific information about your market. Professional market research firms often have the expertise to efficiently and effectively use these methods. You can choose any or all of these methods depending on your goal and the cost-benefit ratio of the research method. Complex consumer research involves more complicated preparation and analysis than the simple research methods mentioned earlier. Complex consumer research includes:

■ Large, in-depth surveys that cover a topic of interest in detail, or several topics covered lightly. These may be given to hundreds or thousands of consumers in your market area.

■ **Focus groups** consist of a face-to-face meeting of customers or potential customers who are asked to react to or comment on a topic of interest (similar to topics in surveys). Focus groups are usually conducted by a third-party facilitator who does not influence the information provided by the group.

- **Test marketing** involves trying out actual products or services on real customers, often in a limited geographic area so as to minimize cost and risk. Most operations have customers try potential menu items by offering them as specials. Test marketing also involves making the test product available to a wider group of consumers. For example, an establishment may offer samples at a shopping mall or a fair.

- **Competitive analysis** involves gathering information about the products, prices, and services of your competitors and drawing conclusions about how they affect your business. A simple competitive analysis can be done by any operation. A more comprehensive one might require professional assistance.

- **Demographic analysis** looks at customer data, such as age, education, socioeconomic group, location, family type, home type, income, etc., from census reports and special research to form customer subgroups. Then the needs and wants of the subgroups can be determined and sales estimates can be made.

Obtaining Feedback from Internal and External Customers

After you have identified internal and external customer expectations and attempted to meet them, you should consistently gather feedback to determine how well those expectations were met.

Feedback from External Customers

External customer feedback seeks to find out a customer's satisfaction with:

- Service times
- Cleanliness
- Service quality
- Menu layout
- Product quality
- Menu selection

You can obtain information about the customer's satisfaction either through face-to-face questioning or through objective methods.

In all cases, employees should be sensitive to how much external customers want to be questioned or probed. You should ensure that all managers and staff with external customer contact can recognize a guest's cues that they do not want to provide feedback. Training can help provide skills in this area.

Face-to-Face Questioning

The easiest and most frequent method of getting external customer feedback is by asking for it. Servers should check back one or two minutes after serving any beverage or food to see whether it is satisfactory; the guest should not be forced to wait very long to report a problem. Frequently, guests will request some small addition such as butter, another utensil, etc. Little things like these, when taken care of quickly, add considerably to customer satisfaction.

The second most popular method of obtaining external customer feedback is having the dining room or operations manager stop at the table to ask how everything is going. This not only gives the guest an opportunity to comment on the food, beverage, and service, but it also gives the guest an opportunity to meet the manager. If this is done frequently, a rapport will build between regular guests and an operation. The manager, especially with regular guests, can discuss areas where changes or improvements can be made. These discussions can cover the food or beverage menu (especially wine and beer), the décor, service, hours, and many other things.

Whatever method you choose, it should be designed to gather specific information. For example, instead of asking a guest "How is your dinner?" ask "Is the steak prepared to your satisfaction?" Similarly, "Is there anything else I can get for you tonight?" could be rephrased to "Thank you for dining with us this evening. How can we make your evening more enjoyable?"

Face-to-face questioning is good for uncovering immediate problems or for getting a rough idea of the level of customer satisfaction. However, people do not usually like to report minor problems or dissatisfactions; they will tend to say that everything is okay. People also tend to say what they think the questioner wants to hear, especially if they think someone will get into trouble because of negative feedback. This means that you should only give moderate weight to this method; if you need more accurate information, then you should also use objective research methods.

Objective Research Methods

As much as possible, objective methods of gathering data should be used. **Objective methods** involve gathering information without using a person whose interpretation or memory of what was said could change the feedback. Any of the objective methods already described for gathering needs and expectations of internal and external customers can be used for gathering feedback. For example, a restaurant might have a customer feedback form on its Web site

Exhibit 3f

Online Dine-In Comments Form

HOME   WELCOME   MENUS   ORDER FOOD   PRIVATE PARTIES   GIFT CERTIFICATES   LOCATION   CONTACT US

175 Hillcrest Dr., Eagle Grove, IL • phone 815.432.1534

Café de la Lune
French Bistro

We Invite Your Comments

Dine-In Comments

Carry-Out Comments

General Comments

Daily Specials

Special Events

Our Family

News Letter Request

Photo Album

Bulletin Board

Dine-in Comment Form; all fields will scroll to accommodate entry.

What was the date of your visit with us?

What was your server's name?

How often do you dine with us?
○ First time
○ Once in a while
○ Regularly

What area of the menu did you select on this visit?
(Check all that apply.)
○ Dinner
○ Pasta
○ Pizza
○ Sandwiches
○ Appetizers
○ Desserts

How do our prices compare to the food and service?
○ Lower than expected
○ About right
○ Overpriced

How would you rate our performance today?

Please use the following scale:
Excellent 4   Good 3   Fair 2   Poor 1

The timeliness of our service:
___ Front desk host(s)
___ Server(s)
___ Bartender(s)
___ Bussers
___ Room host(s)
___ Our courteousness

The timeliness of your meal:
___ Food
___ Beverage

Your food item:
___ Quality
___ Temperature
___ Appearance

Submit

Some operations offer easy ways for customers to provide feedback, such as a form on their Web site.

(see *Exhibit 3f*) that customers can use anonymously; however, customers must be directed to this feedback opportunity.

There are several objective methods available to the restaurant or foodservice operation to gather information about how well they are serving external customers' needs and expectations.

■ **Comment cards** solicit immediate feedback from the guest about the dining experience. (See *Exhibit 3g* on the next page.) Comment cards can take many forms. Cards could be part of the table setting, presented with the guest check, printed on the guest receipt, or available online through your restaurant's Web site. When analyzing comment cards, keep in mind more people will complete a comment card if they have had a poor experience. If the negative comments are random, it may simply indicate a one-time error. However, management should investigate the comment and respond to the guest. Negative comments that are consistent or follow a pattern indicate a more serious problem. In addition to investigating the comment and responding to the guest, management may have to revise a process or

Exhibit 3g

Sample Comment Card

To Our Guests

Our Mission: Every guest who chooses to dine in our restaurant leaves satisfied.

Date Visited: _____ / _____ / _____

Service was prompt and friendly	**Excellent**	**Average**	**Poor**
Product quality	**Excellent**	**Average**	**Poor**
Cleanliness of restaurant	**Excellent**	**Average**	**Poor**

Is there a particular employee you would like to single out for praise?

Would you recommend our restaurant to an acquaintance?   **Yes**   **No**

Other comments: (*Optional*)

_____

_____

(Optional)

Name: _____

Address: _____

City: _____   **State:** _____   **Zip Code:** _____

Phone: _____   **Email:** _____

Well-written comment cards can provide valuable information when completed after a meal.

---

procedure to eliminate the problem. A few additional points of caution about comment cards:

- ☐ Content should be limited and focused.

- ☐ The guests should be able to complete their comments in a short time.

- ☐ Guest personal information is necessary for management to respond.

- ☐ Maintain the comment cards in a file for future reference.

Objective methods can be used along with methods such as customer interaction (both internal and external customers) and observation, staff meetings, and focus groups. However, since objective methods are unbiased in nature, they should be used more frequently.

Larger operations, such as chains, may use more far-reaching methods such as:

- ■ **Mystery shoppers** or **secret shoppers** are consultants or employees who visit an operation, act as normal guests, and secretly report to management on the food, service, facility, and the experience

- ■ A market research firm to telephone customers and get their feedback

- ■ Toll-free numbers for guests to call and discuss their dining experiences

For customers to provide feedback through the phone or a Web site takes effort and time on their part. To encourage customers who take the time to call a toll-free number or respond via a Web site, some operations offer a complimentary meal or discounted entrée. As with comment cards, a higher proportion of people with complaints will provide feedback than those with neutral or positive attitudes. (See *Exhibit 3h.*) Offering a complimentary meal or discounted entrée also may unintentionally discourage negative input.

50

Exhibit 3h

Voluntary Comments

		Customer Opinion of Product or Service						
Likelihood of Voluntary Comments		Outstanding	Excellent	Very Good	Average	Poor	Bad	Awful
	Often				X	X	X	X
	Sometimes	X						
	Rarely		X	X	X			

Voluntary comments tend to be biased toward the negative.

All of these data-gathering methods should be set up so that feedback goes immediately to you in order to quickly correct problems.

Feedback from Internal Customers

For internal customers you should obtain feedback on their satisfaction regarding:

- Scheduling and number of work hours
- Training and development
- Compensation and benefits
- Working conditions
- Processes and procedures
- Tools and equipment

The questioning methods previously described for guests also work for employees. Simply asking employees individually or at a meeting what they like and dislike, what they would change, etc., will tell you a lot. You can also use the objective methods for uncovering internal customers' needs to gather employee feedback.

Analyzing Feedback

Once you gather the feedback, you must analyze the data so that you can improve the situation, menu, food, processes, etc. Failing to analyze and act on feedback could make the situation worse. People do not like to spend time giving feedback only to learn that nothing was done with it. So analysis and action should be part of your plan for gathering feedback.

The goals of analysis are to identify areas that need improvement and to prioritize potential improvements in terms of costs and benefits. Analysis can also indicate areas that could be models to use in other aspects of customer service. External and internal customer feedback is very valuable information that, if used properly, can make the difference between good customer service and exceptional customer service.

Analysis Methods

In most cases, a market research firm or consultant will conduct market research. **Statistical analysis systems (SAS)** are used to tabulate and collate research data. This data is then used to develop a research report. SAS procedures use descriptive analysis methods to analyze data. Descriptive analysis uses data to describe the average or typical respondent and to what degree that respondent varies from the norm. The two most often used analysis methods are *frequencies* and *means.*

The frequencies method tabulates and counts the frequency of responses to each question on a research instrument. Here is a possible research question:

■ How many times in an average month do you dine away from home?

☐ Less than 4 times

☐ 5–10 times

☐ 11–15 times

☐ 16–20 times

☐ More than 20 times

The frequencies method counts how many times or how frequently each of the possible responses is selected. Frequencies can be provided as raw numbers, percentages, a combination of the two, or in a client's customized format.

The means method provides information about the mean, or average number of responses to a variable. Standard deviation of a variable is another data analysis tool that can be determined using the means procedure. A **standard deviation** measures how far a response is from the mean.

Whatever analysis method is used, the first step is usually to count the data. Typically, the data is grouped into useful chunks such as by menu item and time period. This includes time of day, meal period, day of week, month, season, etc. For example, you might have data about the following menu items: hamburgers, pan fish, prime rib, and roast pork. You might find that the most useful time period to track this data is by the day of the week. When counting the results, it is organized in a table as shown in *Exhibit 3i.*

Exhibit 3i

Tabulated Customer Satisfaction Data

Menu Item	Sun		Mon		Tue		Wed		Thu		Fri		Sat	
	Good	Bad	Good	Bad	Good	Bad	Good	Bad	Good	Bad	Good	Bad	Good	Bad
Hamburger	16	7	22	9	18	3	26	1	14	3	28	5	26	8
Pan fish	11	1	18	1	25	2	19	1	22	2	19	6	12	9
Prime rib	47	1	4	24	12	4	19	2	34	2	41	3	44	2
Roast pork	33	3	30	19	18	4	27	2	29	2	36	3	35	1

Although the data is in a table, it can be difficult to understand and use. The easiest way to gain value from the data is to graph it. Graphs are great for tracking trends and cycles and making unusual data noticeable. However, you do not want to graph all of the data in the table; that would be very confusing. Rather, select just the parts you want to think about and graph them. In this case, you want to see how the prime rib does throughout the week at dinner, as illustrated in *Exhibit 3j*.

Exhibit 3j

Prime Rib Customer Satisfaction Graph

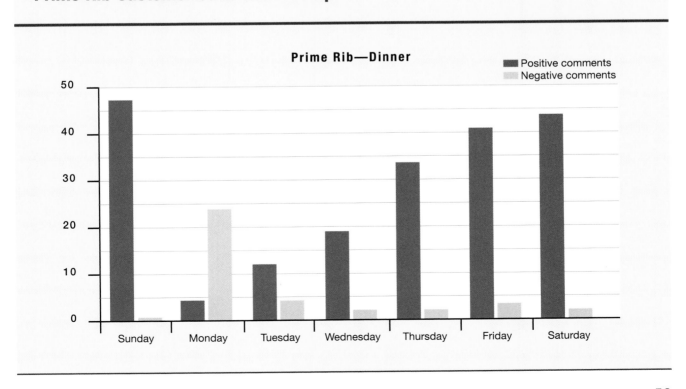

The graph shows that prime rib grows in popularity from Monday through Sunday. However, you also should notice that the bad comments far outweigh the good comments on Monday. This should alert you to some problem with this dish on Monday. When you investigate, you might find that you are serving leftovers from Sunday, and they are not well received. Whatever the reason, you are aware of a potential problem and must find out what it is and fix it.

Activity

We Hear Your Feedback!

Obtain permission from a restaurant or foodservice operation to collect some of their guest comment cards to analyze and discuss in class. Collect these cards over a period of one week or more. The objective is to collect cards that cover each day part (meal period) and day of the week. After reviewing the cards, separate them into any number of categories, such as days of the week, meal period, references to menu, staff, cleanliness, etc. For each category, count the number of positive and negative comments. Keep in mind guests tend to comment when they have not been satisfied, so the ratio of negative to positive comments is not as important as the repeated occurrence of a particular comment.

After categorizing the comment cards, analyze the data. What are the comments telling you about the business? Is there a particular day that seems significant for one reason or another? Is there a theme? What are the positive comments saying? What are the negative comments saying? In some cases, things will be obvious; in others, you may have to really think about it. Do not limit or predetermine what the cards are telling you about the business.

Based on the collected data, try to reach some conclusions. Of these conclusions, develop a list of those conclusions that need improvement and of those that should be modeled. Prepare a report documenting what you did, what you found out, and your interpretations.

Summary

Customer expectations can change often. A properly designed, implemented, and managed high-quality customer service system should have processes in place to continuously monitor and record internal and external customer expectations. The tools and methods for collecting, recording, and analyzing customer service data should also be adjusted over time. The best source of information is the customer. If methods and tools are used properly, both internal and external customers will be very accommodating in providing the valuable feedback necessary to stay current with customer demands and expectations.

Review Your Learning

1 The starting point for developing a process for identifying customer expectations is

    A. the guest.

    B. the mission statement.

    C. internal service quality (in the service-profit chain).

    D. marketing research data from the U.S. census.

2 The "four rights" of internal service quality are

    A. hire, train, compensate, and tolerate.

    B. hire, train, discipline, and retain.

    C. hire, discipline, compensate, and retain.

    D. hire, train, compensate, and retain.

3 The following have been identified as major concerns of the internal customer *except*

    A. meeting manager's demands.

    B. having a good job design.

    C. having the proper tools.

    D. receiving development and training.

4 Communicating employer expectations to potential employees can

    A. lead to a reduction in employee turnover.

    B. lead to increased employee turnover.

    C. be a violation of employee law.

    D. reduce the work of the hiring process.

5 The expectations of the internal customer

    A. are *not* part of the customer satisfaction process.

    B. are the responsibility of the employee.

    C. should be a serious consideration of the operation.

    D. should be a serious consideration of the external customer.

6 Customer service expectations of the external customer

    A. can be influenced by moments of truth.

    B. are determined by chance.

    C. cannot be influenced by the foodservice operation.

    D. None of the above

7 Asking your bartenders how they like the new longer hours on Thursdays is an example of

    A. market research.

    B. getting feedback from external customers.

    C. compensating right.

    D. getting feedback from internal customers.

8 Collecting feedback from the customer should be

    A. everyone's responsibility.

    B. management's responsibility.

    C. a market research firm's responsibility.

    D. a human resources department's responsibility.

9 All of the following are ways to identify staff who can deliver prompt, friendly, and courteous customer service *except*

    A. hiring employees who were referred by present employees.

    B. using the supportive processes of the service-profit chain.

    C. reconsidering recently qualified people who were not hired.

    D. contacting former good employees to see if they might return.

continued on next page

Review Your Learning *continued from previous page*

10 Determining customer's expectations is important because

    A. you need to know what they are in order to satisfy them.

    B. customers want the same things that you want.

    C. employee training must be based on this knowledge.

    D. it is required by law in most states.

11 All of the following are tools for identifying external customer expectations *except*

    A. conversation.

    B. observation and questioning.

    C. job interviews.

    D. demographic analysis.

12 All of the following are tools for identifying internal customer expectations *except*

    A. focus groups.

    B. suggestion boxes.

    C. watching and listening to them during work.

    D. asking for input.

13 Gathering feedback from external customers is important because

    A. customers expect you to do it.

    B. it is required by federal law.

    C. it supports your opinions about dining.

    D. it lets you know how well you are doing.

14 You should obtain all the following types of feedback from internal customers *except*

    A. their satisfaction with suppliers.

    B. their satisfaction with scheduling and hours.

    C. their satisfaction with working conditions.

    D. their satisfaction with tools and equipment.

15 You should obtain all the following types of feedback from external customers *except*

    A. their satisfaction with the service they received.

    B. their satisfaction with the food you served.

    C. their satisfaction with management.

    D. their satisfaction with the facility's cleanliness.

16 All of the following are tools used to obtain guest feedback *except*

    A. face-to-face questioning.

    B. tools and equipment.

    C. comment cards.

    D. mystery shoppers.

17 All of the following are tools used to obtain employee feedback *except*

    A. surveys.

    B. shift meetings.

    C. standard deviation.

    D. one-on-one questioning.

Ensuring Consistent Service Value

4

Inside This Chapter

- ■ Proper and Effective Communication with the Customer
- ■ Guest Satisfaction through Suggestive Selling
- ■ Managing the Pace and Flow of Service
- ■ Service Recovery

After completing this chapter, you should be able to:

- ■ Ensure proper and effective communication with the customer.
- ■ Maximize guest satisfaction through suggestive selling.
- ■ Ensure that products are served promptly, as ordered, and to standards.
- ■ Manage the pace and flow of service.
- ■ Ensure satisfactory resolution of customer complaints.

Test Your Knowledge

1 **True or False:** Service recovery refers to a proper flow of service. *(See p. 74.)*

2 **True or False:** Suggestive selling is a good way to maximize the guest's bill. *(See p. 66.)*

3 **True or False:** It is possible that a sender and a receiver can have effective communication with no overlap in their fields of experience. *(See p. 59.)*

4 **True or False:** Guest complaints are best handled by the manager. *(See p. 74.)*

5 **True or False:** The most important aspect of effective communication is the content of the message. *(See p. 63.)*

Key Terms

Field of experience   Service recovery

Receiver   Suggestive selling

Sender

Think About It...

In your experience, what percentage of internal and external customer complaints can be traced back to miscommunication? What is the primary cause of poor communication in your workplace? How can communication be improved within your workplace?

Introduction

Maximizing both internal and external customers' satisfaction should be the goal of your business. Two critical components of high-quality customer service are service and product consistency, and the customer's feeling of value for what they paid. Once you have identified customer expectations, you must consistently meet or exceed them so customers feel they received high-quality service and got their money's worth. Consistent, high-quality customer service means getting everything right every time. Tools that can help you consistently meet or exceed customer expectations and create value for them include effective communication, managing the flow of business, and resolving conflict.

Proper and Effective Communication with the Customer

Miscommunication happens all the time. In a restaurant or foodservice operation, communication mistakes can lead to errors in customer service, from misunderstanding a request to not recognizing positive feedback.

Activity

The Telephone Game

1 The entire class should line up in a single line; the line can snake around the room if necessary.

2 The person at one end starts the action by writing out a short description of:

☐ A favorite television show

☐ A funny personal experience

☐ Activities done over the weekend

3 This same person whispers the description to the next person in line.

4 The listener, without writing down the description, whispers the same description to the next person in line, and each person continues until the end of the line is reached.

5 The last person to hear the description says it aloud to the entire class.

6 The initiator reads aloud the original description to the entire class.

7 The class discusses the changes that took place as the message was passed along.

The Communication Process

Communication is an extremely complex process. The sender-receiver model (see *Exhibit 4a* on the next page) shows the communication process. The **sender** is the person who has a message to communicate. The **receiver** is the person who gets the sender's message. The sender needs to (a) send the message, and (b) get feedback that it was received accurately. Communication is also affected by the **field of experience,** which consists of all the things a person has gone through that affect either forming or interpreting a message. The sender's field of experience impacts how a message is sent. The receiver's field of experience impacts how a message is received and understood.

Once the message is received, the receiver processes the message with his or her thoughts and feelings. The receiver then forms a new message and reverses roles with the sender. A sender and receiver can communicate more accurately if they have a large overlap in their fields of experience. They will not communicate well if overlap in their fields of experience is small.

Exhibit 4a

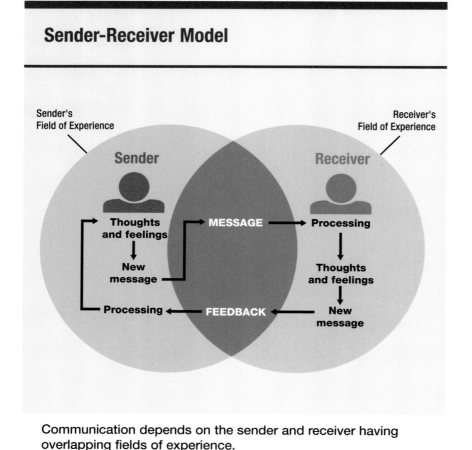

Sender-Receiver Model

Communication depends on the sender and receiver having overlapping fields of experience.

Developed from discussion of communication models in Bormann, Ernest G. *Communication Theory.* New York: Holt, Rinehart, and Winston, 1980.

The following factors can affect a sender's and receiver's fields of experience:

- Culture
- Education
- Past experiences
- Values
- Perceptions
- Assumptions
- Expectations
- Emotions
- Verbal skills
- Nonverbal skills

Here are some examples of miscommunication in an operation:

- A guest asks an employee who is unfamiliar with American slang, "What's hot on your menu tonight?" The employee responds by listing the menu items that are served hot.

- A server recognizes a guest from past visits and assumes that the guest knows the menu items. Therefore, the server does not highlight items that the restaurant wants to promote. As a result, the customer does not consider these items when ordering.

- A manager believes that the line cook has more training and skills than the line cook actually has. The manager asks the line cook to "work on *mise en place*." The line cook does not understand the request but is embarrassed to ask for clarification. Instead, the line cook nods his head. The manager thinks that the line cook understood and accepted the assignment. As a result, the food preparation for the day part is not done.

Clear communication is the solution for these situations. Managers should familiarize employees with common guest questions. A server should be trained to avoid making any assumptions about a guest, even if the guest is a frequent visitor. During the hiring interview, the manager should ask probing questions about a candidate's experience and background.

Restaurant Communication Problems

In addition to the fields of experience, there are many other things that can affect communication. The restaurant and foodservice industry provides jobs to a wide variety of people who are diverse in culture, language, education, and other factors that can affect communication. All these differences can be barriers to accurate communication and can cause communication problems. Common communication barriers include:

- Stereotyping
- Defensiveness
- Relative status of the sender and receiver
- Emotional situation
- Environmental problems (noise, sound absorption, etc.)
- Differences in background or culture
- Poor timing
- Number of messages being received at the same time
- Conflict (differences or disagreement) between messages

Examples of communication problems caused by these barriers include:

- A high-school-age server may be very uncomfortable having a conversation with a figure of authority such as a district manager.

- The kitchen in a busy pizza parlor is a very noisy place. As a result, the cooks sometimes misunderstand food orders.

- The height of the meal hour typically is very busy in a downtown deli, and many people are giving multiple orders to the kitchen in a short period of time. As a result, some of the orders are lost.

- An employee receives conflicting messages from the boss. First, the boss tells the bartender to set up the barware as a priority. A few minutes later, the boss tells the bartender to make clearing the tap lines the priority. As a result, the bartender is not sure what to do first.

As a manager, if you can anticipate these communication barriers ahead of time, you may be able to improve communication by changing a message or holding off on delivering a message until things are calmer to avoid potential conflict between messages. You might also be able to get feedback on messages that were received. If you spot these barriers after communication occurred, you may be able to correct any resulting miscommunication, misunderstanding, or misinformation. You may be able to improve communication and how people feel by praising an employee, or gently pointing out how something should have happened.

Good communication can help:

- Lower costs

- Improve the work environment

- Retain staff

- Satisfy customers

The following example shows how one fine-dining restaurant uses staff meetings as a way to address and communicate important information.

The maitre d'hôtel and the chef of a famous upscale midwestern restaurant require every scheduled staff person to attend a meeting before opening the dining room. The meeting agenda is fairly consistent each day.

1. The maitre d'hôtel reviews any positive and negative service issues from the previous night, such as communication, proper language, and etiquette.

2. The maitre d'hôtel reviews the guest reservations for the evening. If there are any special guests on the reservation list, everyone is made aware of the guest's name, the reservation time, where he or she will be seated, the number in the party, and any special requests. If the special guest is returning, his or her prior experiences are reviewed.

3. The chef reviews and explains the evening menu, including ingredients and items to promote.

4. Everyone is encouraged to ask questions and discuss expectations throughout the staff meeting.

This type of meeting can significantly help to identify and eliminate communication problems.

Good Listening Skills

Sending a message is only half of the communication model; listening (receiving) is the other half. The same fields of experience and barriers apply to receiving messages as to sending them.

Good listening skills are critical. To listen effectively, a person must be interested in what is communicated and pay attention to the sender. The receiver should not interrupt and should let the sender complete the message. In general, follow the principles for effective listening shown in *Exhibit 4b*.

Communication is an interactive process, and doing it effectively depends on a complex set of circumstances.

Exhibit 4b

Principles of Effective Listening

- Prepare to listen.
- Stop talking.
- Pay attention.
- Do not interrupt.
- Practice listening.

Nonverbal Communication

Communication is also nonverbal and includes body language, manner of speech, eye contact, and tone of voice. Also, being patient, showing respect, and treating others with dignity impact the effectiveness of communication.

Techniques for Effective Communication

There are several aspects to being an effective communicator, such as being:

- Credible
- Confident
- Courteous
- Clear
- Concerned

Being Credible

It is important that guests find your staff credible during communication. Credibility and believability are critical when the communication involves solving a problem.

For servers, product knowledge is important to credibility. To be credible with customers, the information they communicate must be accurate. At a minimum, servers should know the menu item descriptions, including specials. Great product knowledge includes preparation techniques, ingredients, allergens, substitutions, and the right combinations of food and drink. With this additional information, a server can present the menu accurately and answer customers' questions. A strong test of credibility occurs when a customer asks about the menu or specific items on it. (See *Exhibit 4c.*) The guest assesses the server's credibility by the knowledge in the server's response. Imagine how a customer feels if a server does not know enough about the menu to answer the question to the customer's expectation.

In another example, chefs must have knowledge of processes and procedures to be credible. The level of knowledge depends on the type of cooking assignment. At a minimum, a chef should be able to describe the correct preparation process or procedure and know how to carry it out. Great cooking knowledge includes knowing the reasons for a process and every step in it, its history or development from earlier methods, and how to compare different but related processes.

When a guest complains about something, the credibility of the server or manager who handles the complaint is critical to good communication. The server must know the operation's policies and procedures for managing complaints, including any allowed

Exhibit 4c

Knowing the menu well will help you be credible to your guests.

adjustments. If the guest senses the server is hesitant, lacks knowledge, or needs to check with someone higher up, the guest may think the server is not credible, and may doubt his or her ability to resolve the complaint.

Being Confident

To be effective communicators, staff must present a confident image to guests, without seeming arrogant. Polite confidence adds to credibility and tells internal and external customers that they can rely on you to meet their expectations and needs. The elements of giving a confident impression include:

- Displaying body language, especially facial expressions, that are consistent with the verbal message
- Showing interest
- Being responsive
- Remaining confident throughout the conversation

Being Courteous

Being courteous is important when communicating, especially when there is a complaint. Do this by:

- Showing respect for the people involved; everyone is entitled to an opinion and personal respect.
- Using titles and surnames when appropriate; if you don't know them, say "sir" and "ma'am" instead.
- Remaining polite.
- Listening to what the other person has to say without prejudging. Wait until you hear all the facts.
- Being patient and letting the speaker have the necessary time to communicate; some people think and speak more slowly than others.
- Speaking and listening to others as you want them to speak and listen to you.

All of these will help create an atmosphere of courtesy and respect.

Being Clear

Many communication problems happen when what is said and what is meant are misunderstood, not from actual differences of opinion.

You can avoid this kind of miscommunication by doing the following:

- Use plain language and avoid using jargon or slang. Although jargon might be part of the staff's normal dialogue, a customer may not know it and could feel confused or uncomfortable.

- Listen carefully to what is being said and how it is being said.

- Use exact and precise language. Indicate what you want as the final result; do not leave this up to the listener to figure out. For example, do not tell the waitstaff to "act in a businesslike manner;" they might not have the same definition of this behavior as you do. Instead, tell the waitstaff to "concentrate on your tasks and avoid too much socializing."

- Check for and confirm understanding on a regular basis. You can do this by repeating in your own words what you heard the other person say and then asking the other person if you heard correctly.

- Summarize the action points to take once you agree that you heard correctly, and confirm that everyone involved understands who will do what and by when.

Being Concerned

It is important to be concerned and ensure the other person sees you as being concerned. This has two aspects:

- When you are concerned and interested in what the other person says, you are likely to pay attention to it, carefully consider it, and start thinking about how to help. (See *Exhibit 4d.*)

- You should also be concerned about the success of the operation and all its activities, including satisfying customers, being profitable, having a good reputation, etc. This allows you to take operational goals into consideration in your communication.

When you communicate this way, others will pay more attention to your messages, and you will pay more attention to theirs, with more mutual respect. This results in better communication all around and enables everyone to be responsive to others' needs. A good way to reinforce excellent communication techniques is to practice scenarios and role-plays during preshift or regular staff meetings. You can use previous guest complaints as the scenarios, then ask the staff what they would do differently. Also, you can use your knowledge of common guest issues to create scenarios for staff input.

Exhibit 4d

It is important to show interest and concern when listening to guests.

Activity

Handling Miscommunication

In small groups of three to five people, share a situation from each person's work or dining experience that involved a communication issue (either positive or negative). Each group must choose one experience to discuss with the class. The group should describe the situation, the people involved, and what made it a positive experience, or what could have been changed to make it positive.

Guest Satisfaction through Suggestive Selling

The output of the employee satisfaction process leads to the employee productivity process. One aspect of employee productivity is how well employees sell. Suggestive selling is a large part of employee sales and productivity.

Suggestive selling involves recommending additional or different items to a customer. It is one of the keys to the success of any retail business. In a restaurant, suggestive selling should maximize guest satisfaction and increase the average check, resulting in increased profitability. The success of suggestive selling depends on having the right people with product knowledge, effective communication skills, and sales training to sell to guests.

Many employees are reluctant to suggestive sell because they are shy, or they think that suggestive selling makes them too pushy, or they are uncomfortable with selling. All these reasons for hesitating to suggestive sell can be handled with proper training. Even so, it is a good practice to hire waitstaff and bartenders who are willing to suggestive sell.

Training Employees to Suggestive Sell

Managers who train servers to suggestive sell commonly point out that it will increase the guest's check and the tip. However, suggestive selling involves a lot more than just selling additional menu items.

The customer service approach encourages more servers to suggestive sell. In this approach, suggesting an appetizer, side dish, or dessert is used to actually enhance the guest's dining experience and maximize guest satisfaction. (See *Exhibit 4e.*) This approach has been extremely effective in training restaurant employees to suggestive sell.

Exhibit 4e

Suggestive selling can enhance the guest's dining experience.

A good suggestive selling training program should include:

■ Enhancing servers' communication skills so they can be effective with customers

■ Developing servers' product knowledge so they can vividly and accurately describe items to customers, as well as mention ingredients that may cause allergic reactions

■ Learning the items that complement each other so they can be suggested to customers

■ Anticipating guest needs so servers can be ready with suggestions

■ Suggesting add-on items such as drinks, appetizers, and desserts

■ Suggesting specific items; for example, "Would you like lemonade on this hot day?" rather than asking, "Would you like something to drink?"

■ Suggesting items that servers themselves enjoy

■ Suggesting core products and services that sell well

■ Suggesting the establishment's best items to increase the probability that the customer will be happy with them

■ Using props such as dessert trays

■ Observing customer behavior to determine whether they want service or a product, for example, at the end of the meal, watching the guest to see if he or she wants the check or dessert

■ Discussing the effect that suggestive selling has on the financial position of the restaurant

Management should make suggestive selling training an ongoing effort. First, training can be conducted formally by a manager or a designated trainer. Second, suggestive selling can be an occasional agenda item for staff meetings. You can set aside time at staff meetings to discuss the best practices or problem experiences. Third, informal training can occur through observation and feedback. In all cases, practice is key to successful suggestive selling.

Incentives for Suggestive Selling

In addition to taking a customer service approach to encourage suggestive selling, you can also use incentives and contests. For example:

■ Reward servers who sell the most.

■ Give sellers a commission for selling non-entrée items such as appetizers and desserts.

■ Hold sales contests that reward employees for selling the most of certain menu items.

These programs work well, but there are also some challenges when using them. You must be cautious when implementing incentive programs. It can be difficult to design incentives and contests that are fair to all servers on all shifts. Also, you must avoid creating a culture where servers only suggestive sell when there is an incentive or other reward.

Once your servers and bartenders have sold as much as is reasonable, the challenge of customer service shifts to delivering food and beverages in ways that will please the customer.

Managing the Pace and Flow of Service

Wait, service, cook, and callback times are all timing issues that are very important in the restaurant and foodservice industry. For quick-service, full-service, and fine-dining restaurants, managing the pace and flow of service is all about timing. In a quick-service environment, it is important to get the guest through the dining process as quickly as possible without being rude. In a fine-dining environment, the objective is to create a smooth and elegant culinary experience that leaves the guest with a pleasurable memory.

All restaurant and foodservice operations have a service system that involves timing. Some systems may be simple, and others very complex. The important thing is to set standards for all aspects of guest services, especially those affecting the pace and flow of service, such as:

■ Reservations

■ Staff demeanor

■ Greeting and seating procedures

■ Preparation and presentation of food and drink products

- Dining room arrangement and setup

- Table setup and place settings

- Specials explanations

- Order taking

- Suggestive selling

- Food and drink delivery and placement

- Ongoing attention to guests' needs

- Beverage replenishment

- Used table service and remaining food pickup, including "doggie bags"

- Guest check presentation

- Payment acceptance and processing

- Goodbyes

The next step is to actually meet all of these standards.

The Systems Management Approach

Recall from Chapter 2 that a systems management approach looks at the activities in your operation as a group of different processes and tasks that work together to meet the objectives of each process and the whole operation. To effectively manage the service system, you must be aware of activities in all guest services aspects of the entire operation. For example:

- A backup in the kitchen may have been caused by seating too many guests in a short period of time for the number of kitchen staff on hand.

- Longer than expected wait times for seating may be due to guests lingering in the dining room after completing their meals or by slow check delivery and payment processing.

- No-shows, equipment breakdowns, large groups, etc., can all be the cause of many pace and flow problems.

Using the systems management approach, if the service system is designed, implemented, and staffed properly, problems will last a short time. If a problem continues, you must examine the components of your system to find the problem and any impacted areas. These components include process, staffing, support, equipment, production, etc. No matter how insignificant something may seem, it should not be overlooked. Make an effort to find the problem and then take action to solve it.

Properly Receiving and Recording Reservations and Special Requests

One of the more frustrating things a customer experiences is a lost or incorrect reservation or special request. If a customer's visit starts with this kind of error, it can be difficult to turn the visit into a positive experience. That is why it is extremely important to have an accurate system that records reservations and special requests and that implements them at the right time.

Exhibit 4f

It is important to have an accurate system for recording reservations and special requests.

First, you must have an effective procedure, including a place for recording reservations and special requests. The type, speed, and complexity of the operation determines how sophisticated the procedure is or what technology is used. For example, a fine-dining restaurant with table service may record reservations and special orders in a book or computer at the greeter's station. (See *Exhibit 4f.*) There should only be one place for records to be saved. There should also be a standard for the information recorded, including how and by whom it should be recorded. Then, you must consistently follow the operation's procedure in order for it to work.

The information recorded must be enough to

- Implement the order.

- Identify the guest party upon arrival.

- Confirm the reservation or special order with the guests before they arrive.

- Resolve any problems with the reservation or special order.

In fact, confirming all reservations and special orders is good customer service, makes the guest feel important, and protects the establishment against no-shows. You can confirm by telephone, fax, email, or the style that works for your establishment.

Once the reservation or special order is recorded, there must be a system to communicate this information to staff. First, you must link the reservations and orders to the proper day and time. You can have separate pages for each day, meal, and time slot, or some other form of organization. The reservation or special-order recording procedure must include checking for conflicts with prior reservations and checking for food availability. Then, table setup requirements must be given to the dining room staff, and food or drink requirements must be given to the kitchen staff. The staff must be given this information with enough time to complete the requests. In some establishments, the POS system can communicate this information.

Sometimes, you can preassign special requests to specific cooks, servers, or staff in dining room sections that are capable of handling the request. For example:

- A guest who communicates in sign language must be assigned to a server who can also do this.

- A request for a kosher meal must be assigned to a cook certified to prepare kosher meals.

- A guest who is limited to a wheelchair must be assigned to a table or room that can best accommodate a wheelchair.

With special requests, it is important to have a way to "flag" or call the special request to the attention of cooks, service staff, or others to avoid errors.

Taking reservations and completing special requests seem like simple tasks, but they actually take a lot of planning and organization. With proper planning, establishments can avoid making mistakes in these situations and thus can avoid disappointing guests.

Ensuring Products Are Served Promptly, as Ordered, and to Standards

Guests' expectations, when they place food and drink orders, are for more than just having hot food served hot and cold food served cold. Guests also expect and should receive the following:

- They get what they ordered.

- The order is served promptly without undue delay.

- The food looks appetizing.

- The food tastes the way they expect from the menu description or prior experiences.

Your operation must have a system of standards and procedures to meet these expectations. Some useful techniques in a system are:

■ When guests are seated, have the server make some observations. If they are dressed as though they may be going to another event after the meal, the server may want to ask whether they have any time requirements.

■ Informing guests of any menu items that may take longer to prepare.

■ Repeating orders back to customers after they are taken.

■ Having an effective and efficient system for delivering orders to the kitchen and bar.

■ Adjusting the pace of service to meet guests' expectations. Guests tend to set their own pace. Servers should be trained to observe this and adjust service times as needed.

Some guests may want a quicker pace and others may want a slower one. The key is to routinely observe the guests' own pace and act accordingly, as in the following examples:

■ Communicating regularly with guests while their meals are being prepared to let them know when the food should arrive.

■ Providing kitchen and dining room staff with visual standards of what each entrée plate should look like.

■ Training kitchen and dining room staff to recognize when each entrée plate meets standards.

■ Using an expediter during busy shifts to check the presentation, accuracy, and quality of each order.

■ Having an effective and efficient system to get food and drinks to the table. This system may be different during busy times from a system designed for slower times.

■ Verifying with guests that they received the correct orders.

■ Checking with guests after they have had time to try their food and drinks to ensure that everything is satisfactory.

Exhibit 4g describes a real-life experience that demonstrates two points:

■ The effects of changes in a business flow

■ How management can overlook flaws in a system they assume works well

Exhibit 4g

A Real-Life Example

A resort in northern Minnesota became so successful that the dining room capacity was doubled. The owner hired and trained more staff, purchased additional china and flatware, and seemed to anticipate every issue. However, at peak periods the dining room kept running short of china, glassware, and flatware. Managers analyzed the system, checked inventories, examined service times, and looked at scheduling, but found nothing that could be causing the problems. They decided to wait and see if the shortages worked themselves out, but they did not. Guest complaints increased, the staff became angry with management for not solving the problem, and the bottom line was suffering.

Frustrated and upset, management believed that the problem was in the dishwashing process. They saw that the tables were getting bussed; there was plenty of inventory, and during every peak period, stacks of dirty dishes were seen at the dish sink. However, management chose *not* to take seriously a complaint made by all the dishwashers that the dishwashing machine could not keep up with the increased number of dishes. Instead, management made regular visits to the dish room to make sure the dishwashers were actually washing the dishes they received.

No matter what management tried, the problems continued. Finally, the owners hired consultants to solve the problem. The consultant team arrived at the restaurant, conducted interviews, conducted workflow analysis, and observed the rush periods. After two days, the team submitted their report. The report summarized the team's activities and showed the data to support their conclusion, which was that the dishwashing machine did not have the capacity to handle the increased volume of business. They recommended that a dishwasher with a higher capacity be installed to solve the problem.

This example shows that sometimes it is easy to overlook something obvious. If you look carefully and objectively, you can find the problem. To successfully manage the pace and flow of service, nothing should be taken for granted.

A good tool to use when analyzing pace and flow issues is a flowchart of your processes. (See *Exhibit 4h* on the next page.) By mapping out the flow of service, including who does what tasks and how long the task takes, you can more easily identify any flaws in the system.

Even with good communication and control over the pace and flow of service, mistakes could happen that will leave customers dissatisfied. That is why in order to provide high-quality customer service, you must also handle customer complaints well.

Exhibit 4h

Dishwashing Flowchart

Who	What	Time (minutes)
Buser	Bus table	1
Buser	Put dishes into bus bin	1
Buser	Carry bus bin to dish room	1
Buser	Stack dishes by dishwasher	1
Dish Crew	Load dishwasher	3
Dishwashing Machine	Wash dishes	12
Dish Crew	Remove dishes	3
Dish Crew	Return dishes to service	2
	TOTAL	**24**

A flowchart can help you and your staff understand and clearly identify processes and any flaws.

Service Recovery

You have often heard the expression, "the customer is always right." However, this is not always true. To customers, though, this is completely true, which is why they complain when they are dissatisfied. **Service recovery** refers to an operation's response to a complaint to return to a state of customer satisfaction.

Managers often find that customer complaints are the result of poor communication. Based on the amount of information the customer has at the time, their problem or complaint is probably valid. Providing the customer with a thorough explanation of the menu, ensuring that new customers are familiar with how the establishment operates, and training all employees to consistently communicate information to customers will help minimize communication errors and complaints and speed service recovery.

Characteristics of Successful Operations

Even with excellent communication, some customer complaints and problems can occur. Organizations with a reputation for excellent service recovery have the following characteristics:

- There are standards and guidelines for each specific type of situation.

- The entire staff are trained on how to handle customer complaints.

- The staff have a high level of product knowledge.

- The first staff member who is made aware of the complaint is considered its "owner."

- An environment exists where staff are empowered and trusted to do what is right for the customer and the organization.

Overall Recommendations

Other important factors to help ensure complaints are resolved include:

- Establish a clear policy of who is responsible for handling complaints on each shift. Some operations choose the on-duty manager or shift supervisor. Others set a policy that the person receiving the complaint is its "owner" and is responsible for handling it. In this case, however, a manager should intervene at some point and determine the appropriate solution. (See *Exhibit 4i*.)

- Support employees' decisions when you authorize them to resolve complaints. This develops the needed trust for empowered employees. If the employee's decisions could be improved, you

Exhibit 4i

The person receiving a complaint may be its "owner," but there should be a point where a manager determines the appropriate solution.

should respectfully make the employee aware of a more appropriate solution. Do this either in group training or in private, depending on the sensitivity of the situation and the employee.

How to Handle Guest Complaints

There are proven ways to handle complaints from guests, such as:

- Listen to the guest using your best listening skills.

- Treat the guest with courtesy and respect.

- Be patient.

- Empathize with the guest.

- Paraphrase what you think the problem is to confirm it with the guest. Do this by saying in your own words what you heard and describe the main details.

- Take responsibility for the situation as a manager or employee.

- Take ownership for resolving complaints.

- Offer a solution, explain to the guest what you can do to resolve the problem, or ask the guest how he or she wants the complaint to be resolved.

- Thank the guest for being patient and request his or her future business.

- Thank the guest for his or her concern and for bringing the issue to your attention. Describe how the guest's communication on this and future issues is appreciated.

- Recognize that each guest's situation is different, so there should only be a framework for reimbursement in each situation, and not a written policy.

Exhibit 4j

Handling Customer Complaints

Do	Don't
■ Develop a written communication procedure for addressing complaints that are reported through company mail, email, or other means.	■ Argue with the customer.
	■ Embarrass the customer.
■ Document how different complaints are resolved so employees learn from these real experiences.	■ Accept responsibility verbally, or in writing, for a customer's injury or damage to property until properly investigated, and if necessary, insurance companies are contacted.
■ Identify standards and guidelines for specific complaint situations.	
■ Develop standard apology letters.	
■ Determine reimbursement guidelines for each situation.	

Additional Tips

In addition to all the previous recommendations, *Exhibit 4j* shows more proven techniques for handling customer complaints.

Staff Training

To reinforce product and service knowledge, some organizations regularly test staff on the menu, service issues, how to deal with customer complaints, operational issues, and other aspects of the business. Training for most service recovery plans should include all the points listed in the sections "How to Handle Guest Complaints" and "Additional Tips."

Employees should practice their service recovery skills on a regular basis. Staff meetings are a good time to discuss and practice handling customer complaints. You can take a few actual complaints and conduct a brief role-play where one employee acts as the customer and the other as the employee. Afterward, ask the staff if the complaint was handled well, or how the complaint could have been handled differently.

When training in service recovery, you should address safety, security, and liability concerns and policies, and you should also practice:

■ Listening

■ Being polite and empathetic

■ Being genuine

■ Acknowledging customer concerns

■ Fixing the situation in the best way possible within your powers

■ Recognizing when situations cannot be fixed and apologizing appropriately

Activity

Customer Complaint Role-Play

Use five volunteers to role-play the following service recovery situation. Decide how to best handle the service recovery situation and act out the solution.

Roles

■ Manager

■ Server

■ Buser

■ Customer A (with a complaint)

■ Customer B (seated at the next table)

Situation

Customer A has a complaint about the degree of doneness for a steak entrée. Customer A cannot get the server's attention and complains to the buser. The buser explains that he or she is "just the buser" and tells Customer A that the server has to take care of the problem. By the time Customer A finally gets the server's attention, he or she is very angry.

Actions

■ Customer A explains the problem very loudly to the server.

■ The server tries to resolve the issue.

■ As the server is trying to resolve the issue, Customer B starts complaining to the server that the noise is disturbing his dining experience and requests to see the manager.

■ The server signals the manager to come over and help.

■ The manager discusses the complaints with Customer A and Customer B.

Debrief

Critique the role-play, discuss what the participants did well, and suggest what could have been done differently.

If all the policies and procedures are in place, and all employees are thoroughly trained, your operation can successfully handle customer complaints and recover from them.

Summary

Delivering consistent customer service and creating value help lead to the customer satisfaction and customer loyalty components in the service-profit chain. Communication, suggestive selling, flow of service, and service recovery are tasks that support consistent customer service and creation of value.

Communication is a complex activity and there are many factors involved with effective communication. Many service issues are the result of miscommunication, which can be caused by misunderstanding and other factors. Communication is a two-way process of sending and receiving information, and listening is an important aspect of communication. Staff training to ensure effective communication is management's responsibility. Regular training at staff meetings and preshift meetings can be effective methods to reinforce communication techniques.

Guests want to maximize their dining experience. The staff should help achieve this. Suggestive selling is one tool servers have to enhance a guest's dining experience and meet or exceed expectations. Pace and flow of service is a factor that influences a customer's perception of value. Your operation should have a system of standards and procedures for ensuring that products are served promptly, as ordered, and to standards. The more effectively customers are served, the more they feel their time is respected and appreciated.

Correctly and courteously handling customer complaints and service recovery are critical aspects of customer service. Customers are likely to be more loyal if their complaints are resolved in a satisfactory way. This reinforces the fact that it is in the best interests of both customers and management to resolve complaints positively.

Review Your Learning

1 For the best chances of effective communication between a sender and a receiver, their fields of experience

A. must be completely separate.

B. should have a lot of overlap.

C. should have very little overlap.

D. have no effect on communication.

2 All of the following are barriers to effective communication *except*

A. stereotyping.

B. poor timing.

C. environmental issues.

D. shared fields of experience.

3 On a visit to her favorite tapas restaurant, Tricia was pleasantly surprised to get the warm items she ordered, just the way she likes them, within ten minutes of placing the order. This is an example of how the restaurant

A. properly received and recorded a reservation.

B. made sure that meals are served promptly, as ordered, and to standards.

C. used suggestive selling.

D. used a systems management approach to address food preparation.

4 An important factor in establishing a feeling of confidence is

A. product knowledge.

B. speaking forcefully.

C. questioning the details of the customer's complaint.

D. anticipating a solution before the customer makes a complaint.

5 Siegfried is an experienced server discussing the menu with his guests. While a guest is speaking, Siegfried notices that Todd, another server, is making faces at him from across the room. Siegfried begins to laugh at Todd. Siegfried's communication mistake was that he did *not*

A. share the guest's field of experience.

B. send nonverbal communication to Todd.

C. appear confident by knowing about the products on the menu.

D. properly listen by taking an interest in the guest's comments.

6 To build credibility when dealing with a guest, what should a server use when describing a menu item?

A. Industry jargon

B. Plain language

C. Acronyms

D. Abbreviations

7 An effective way to encourage servers to suggestive sell is to explain that

A. the more they sell, the higher their tip.

B. it is company policy and their performance evaluation may be impacted.

C. suggestive selling is a method of enhancing the guest's dining experience.

D. suggestive selling is a way to upsell customers without their suspecting.

continued on next page

Review Your Learning *continued from previous page*

8 All of the following affect the pace and flow of service *except*

A. staffing.

B. training.

C. special requests.

D. being confident.

9 Service recovery is

A. the time it takes to return to a state of customer satisfaction after a service mistake.

B. an industry term describing service times from first placing an order to its successful completion.

C. the time it takes to recover from a power outage, including restarting all the equipment and reheating all meals in process.

D. an industry term describing an operation's response to a guest complaint.

10 Which of the following is a key factor in resolving a guest complaint?

A. Accepting responsibility for property damage

B. Supporting the employee's decision on how to resolve the complaint

C. Suggesting that the guest may want to order something different next time

D. Having a manager solve all service problems

Ensuring Profit

After completing this chapter, you should be able to:

- Demonstrate the proper use of payment procedures.
- Describe security issues dealing with credit or debit card payment.
- Explain point-of-sale issues affecting profit.
- Explain operational and cost-control issues for to-go, delivery, and drive-through orders.

Test Your Knowledge

1. **True or False:** Employee satisfaction contributes to profit. *(See p. 83.)*

2. **True or False:** These days, checks are very commonly presented as payment for restaurant meals. *(See p. 87.)*

3. **True or False:** Checking customer identification is an important step in processing credit or debit cards. *(See p. 90.)*

4. **True or False:** Cash handling procedures should be the same as credit or debit card handling procedures. *(See p. 85.)*

5. **True or False:** A credit or debit card abuser should be identified at the time of payment. *(See p. 92.)*

Key Terms

Cash overage	Forms of payment
Cash shortage	Reconciliation
Cost ratio	Void

Think About It...

A restaurant is very popular. The food is prepared and presented professionally. Staff are well trained, and revenue is high, yet the restaurant goes out of business in less than a year. This scenario is played out over and over in the restaurant and foodservice industry. Why?

Introduction

There is more to ensuring the profitability of a business than just collecting money. Many restaurant and foodservice establishments generate hundreds of thousands, even millions, of dollars in sales, and yet they fail. One of the reasons they fail is poor money and property management. To do a good job of this, your operation must collect all the money that is due from sales. In addition, you must ensure that:

- All properly collected cash gets into the register.

- No cash in the register leaves illegally.

- You do not lose money as a result of dishonored checks, bad credit, or debit payments.

  - ☐ All personal checks received in payment will be honored by the bank.

  - ☐ All credit or debit card transactions will be honored by the card company.

Review of Financial and Profitability Concepts

The following concepts are critical to your understanding of profitability:

- Two factors that contribute to profit are revenue and costs.

    - *Revenue* is the money generated by sales.

    - *Costs* are the expenses incurred as a result of conducting business. Costs are divided into variable costs and fixed costs.

- *Profit* is the difference between the total sales (or revenue) and the total costs (or expenses.) If sales are higher than costs, the operation makes a profit. However, if total costs are higher than sales, then the operation has incurred a loss.

For a restaurant to be profitable, it must generate revenue and control costs. For example, a restaurant that generates revenue of $1,000,000 but has costs of $1,500,000 is not profitable; it is operating at a loss of $500,000.

The main source of revenue is sales. To ensure that your revenue results in profits, you must establish and control cost ratios. A **cost ratio** is the relationship of an operating cost to another financial figure. The cost ratios of primary interest in the restaurant business are the food cost ratio and the labor cost ratio (also known as the food cost percentage and the labor cost percentage). The food cost ratio is the percentage of sales that is spent on food supplies; this ratio can be calculated for all food or for a single menu item. For example, a steak dinner has a food cost of $5.92 and sells for $17.95; the ratio of cost to price is 33 percent. The remaining 67 percent of revenue for the steak dinner covers other expenses that the restaurant has and, with good planning, leaves a profit. If the food cost ratio gets higher, the amount left for profit is smaller. This is why the food cost ratio must be managed.

Similarly, the labor cost ratio is the percentage of revenue that is spent on the labor to generate the revenue. It works exactly the same way as the food cost ratio, and it also must be managed so that profit can be realized.

To ensure the proper amount of revenue based on sales, you should have accurate payment processing procedures which are discussed later in this chapter.

Review of Customer Service Concepts

In addition to the above financial concepts, the following customer service concepts are critical to understanding how to deal with customers and their relationship to money and profits:

- **High-Quality Customer Service**—Consistently meet or exceed customer expectations by providing products and services that create value for the customer and profit for the organization.

- **The Service-Profit Chain**—Simply stated, if you satisfy internal customers (employees), they will satisfy external customers (guests), thus creating customer loyalty, resulting in an increase in revenue and profit.

This chapter concentrates on the profit aspect of these customer service concepts.

Exhibit 5a

Collecting the payment alone is not enough to be profitable.

Proper Procedures for Accepting Payment

Proper procedures for accepting payment are critical to the profitability of an operation. Using proper procedures for all **forms of payment**—cash, check, money order, credit or debit card, gift certificate, etc.—is necessary. The exact procedure to use will depend on the form of payment.

The critical part of accepting payment is not collecting it, but getting it to the register and recording it. (See *Exhibit 5a.*) Establishing, training, and enforcing the proper procedures for money collection is your responsibility as a manager. If employees handle money in any form, then you must ensure that they are trained before they do so. Mistakes made while learning on the job are very costly to the establishment. Also, you should regularly spot check for proper procedures to identify misunderstandings, shortcuts, errors, improper procedures, and fraud.

Training is crucial to ensuring that sales result in accurately collected and recorded revenue. Training for proper payment acceptance procedures is not just for cashiers. Servers must accurately record and charge for products and services rendered, correctly total the guest check, accept the payment from guests, and return their change. If the guest check is incomplete or wrong, the employee might collect the wrong amount from the guest. If this happens, the guest has underpaid, and the revenue will probably never be recovered.

Exhibit 5b

It is important to handle cash payments correctly.

Handling Cash Payments

In today's business environment, cash payments are becoming less common. Even quick-service establishments now accept credit or debit cards. As a result, employees do not handle cash as frequently and will need cash handling training. Cash handling skills such as counting change, dealing with bills larger than $20, correcting or cancelling payments, and avoiding frauds such as quick-change artists should be part of the training. (See *Exhibit 5b.*) In addition, procedures should be developed, and staff should be trained for special situations such as robbery, dealing with quick-change artists, and other risk management issues.

It is important to properly handle cash payments from customers. Here is a good procedure to follow.

1. When you are paid in cash:
   - ☐ Count the cash.
   - ☐ Make sure that the amount covers the guest check.
   - ☐ Ask the customer if he or she needs change.

2. Place the cash and guest check in a secure carrying device, such as the folder for the check, and carry them to the point-of-sale (POS) system or cash register.

3. Follow the cash processing procedures for your cash register or POS system. These will differ by the type of POS system and for each operation. It is important that both the guest check amount and the payment amount match in the system.

4. Put any change into the folder, carry it back to the table, and return it to the person paying the check.

5. Thank the customer for his or her business, and complete the remaining goodbye protocol of your operation.

6. Walk away from the table so the guest can leave a tip in private.

Handling Voids

When a cashier makes a mistake such as ringing in a wrong amount or item, or a customer changes his mind about something after the electronic transaction has begun, the cashier needs to remove or void it from the computer system or register. A **void** is when a cash register entry has to be corrected by canceling the entry and entering the correct item.

In a line-item void, the payment has not been processed yet, but items have been rung up. Cashiers can either void this themselves, or a manager must enter a code or use a key that allows an item to be removed or changed in the transaction. Voids should be monitored by dollar amount, shift, and cashier. These and other security measures help prevent removing items from a guest check and taking money for them anyway.

Another type of void occurs when an entire transaction must be removed from the system after it has already been completely processed, including the payment. A manager must do this, since the threat of theft is even greater. If the entire transaction is voided because of a mistake or change of mind, typically a new transaction must be entered with the correct information.

Cash Register Practices

An operation should establish a standard payment handling process for cash, checks, and credit cards. Training staff members who collect payments to follow the same process will reduce errors and help identify flaws in the process or staff mistakes. This section and the next discuss a typical cash payment handling process after the customer has paid. The following two sections describe typical handling processes for checks and credit cards.

A cash handling process may include:

Exhibit 5c

Cashiers should only handle one transaction at a time.

- Establish a cash drawer amount based on average check size, ease of replenishing the drawer, and proportion of guests who pay with cash, among other factors.

- Reduce the amount of cash in the register periodically to the established amount.

- Limit cash register access.

- Instruct staff to immediately notify management of any suspicious activity.

- Exchange and balance the cash drawer at every shift change.

- Instruct staff to complete each transaction before beginning another. (See *Exhibit 5c.*) For example, if a guest requests change for a $20 bill while paying for a meal, the payment transaction should be completed before making change.

- Close the cash drawer between transactions and when not in use.

- Take periodic cash register readings to record net sales amounts.

- Some operations require management to approve payments for bills larger than $20.

Cash Overages and Cash Shortages

Tracking cash overages and shortages helps identify problems with cash handling skills. A **cash overage** occurs when you have more cash in the drawer than the POS system or register says you should have. Too many cash overages are a "red flag" that something serious may be happening, since a cash overage results when the guest has probably been shortchanged. They may also be the result of incorrect voids.

A **cash shortage** occurs when there is not enough cash in the registers once they have been reconciled with sales. A large or regular cash shortage would most likely happen from not knowing proper procedures, carelessness, or theft. Poor accounting practices are possible, but that just means the math is wrong, not that cash is being lost. Once you have eliminated accounting errors, you must determine whether the cause is lack of knowledge, carelessness, or theft. If lack of knowledge or carelessness is the cause, then you should retrain employees.

However, if theft is the suspected cause, it can be very difficult to prove unless someone is caught in the act, particularly if there is no established and enforced cash register process. The best prevention is having a consistent cash register process. If the cash register process is enforced, this type of theft can be discouraged.

A one-time cash shortage may be the result of a quick-change artist who tries to confuse the employee while he or she is making change. Proper cash handling procedures will prevent this fraud. That is why management should train staff on cash handling procedures, how to deal with suspicious transactions, and when law enforcement personnel should be informed of suspected activity.

In any event, you should recognize that frequent cash overages and cash shortages are an indicator that additional training or a change in cash handling procedures may be needed.

Handling Payment by Personal Check

Staff members who receive payments should also be trained on handling payment by personal check. The fact that checks are being used less frequently makes this training more important.

Personal check handling practices may include:

- Accept checks only for the amount of the purchase.

- Checks must have the guest's current address and phone number printed on them.

■ Do not accept temporary, second-party, or payroll checks.

■ Two forms of identification must be provided.

■ Once accepted, all checks must be immediately stamped with the bank deposit stamp.

■ Establish a policy for out-of-area checks.

Management is responsible for policies and procedures for accepting checks. The following is a typical procedure for a payment by check.

1 When the personal check is offered as payment:

　□ Verify that the amount covers the guest check amount.

　□ Verify the check is signed.

　□ Ask for two picture IDs and compare the picture and signature with the customer's.

　□ Ask if any change is needed.

2 Take the personal and guest checks in a secure and private carrying device, such as the check folder, to the POS system or cash register.

3 When processing the personal check payment:

　□ Keep the personal and guest checks near each other, and with you.

　□ Do not let others see the personal check account number.

4 Follow the personal check processing procedures for your cash register or POS system. It is important that both the guest check and the payment amounts match in the system.

5 Put any change into the folder, carry it back to the table, and return it to the person paying the check.

6 Thank the customer for his or her business and complete the remaining goodbye protocol of your operation.

7 Leave the table so the guest can leave a tip in private.

Issues that commonly occur when dealing with checks include:

■ Out-of-town checks

■ Second-party checks

■ Identification verification

Your operation's procedures for these issues should be thoroughly covered in staff training. In addition to training staff on check payment policies and procedures, guests should also know your check payment policies. This is typically done with a sign near the cash register or through a notice on the menu. In establishing the check payment policy, you should be sensitive to your target market. An outright policy of not accepting any checks may offend some guests. For example, an operation such as a roadside diner will have a large transient market. A policy allowing only local checks could turn away customers and reduce revenue.

Exhibit 5d

Credit cards and debit cards have become popular forms of payment.

Handling Payment by Credit or Debit Cards

Credit or debit cards are quickly becoming the preferred form of payment in restaurant and foodservice operations. (See *Exhibit 5d.*) In general, the three areas of credit or debit card payment that need to be addressed are:

- Credit or debit card handling procedures at the point of purchase
- Credit or debit card reconciliation
- Dealing with "not approved" or "denied" cards

You should have software and equipment meant for credit or debit card payment at the point-of-sale location. This is essential to implementing card payment policies and procedures. Usually, the POS system defines the procedure for accepting card payments. You can incorporate the POS system's documents and procedures into your training program. Training should include the process for collecting and documenting card data and the data that management will need to reconcile the card transactions.

Many operations use the following POS practices; however, a particular restaurant chain or franchise may have specific variations.

1. Identify form of payment as credit or debit card.

2. Swipe the guest's card.

3. Verify the card number with the numbers displayed onscreen.

4. Enter the charge amount into the POS system (at this point, most systems will automatically request approval).

5. Once the amount is approved, charge slips will print. One is for the guest to sign and leave with the operation (merchant copy) and the other is a receipt for the guest to keep.

6. After the guest has signed the merchant copy, re-enter the POS system and verify the card number.

7. Enter the tip amount.

8. Verify the correct payment amount.

9. Keep the signed card slip for the end-of-shift closeout.

Regardless of the procedure for actually charging the meal to the credit or debit card, there are important overall handling procedures to follow for the card payment.

1 When the card is offered as payment:

☐ Verify that it is signed.

☐ Keep in mind whose card was offered; it may not be the person to whom you gave the guest check.

☐ Ask the customer for his or her zip code; you will use this when processing the card for additional verification.

☐ Ask for a picture ID and compare the picture to the customer, if your establishment has had problems with customers using stolen credit or debit cards.

2 Take the card and guest check in a secure and private carrying device, such as the check folder, to the POS system or card swiper.

3 When processing the card payment:

☐ Keep the card and guest check near each other and with you.

☐ Do not let others see the card number.

☐ Swipe the card and avoid keying in the card number if at all possible. Keying in the card number increases the card company's charges to your operation. If many cards do not properly swipe and must be keyed in, the swipe slot may need cleaning.

☐ Add the zip code to the card information (typically possible only through a POS system). This adds extra verification information and reduces the card company's charges to your operation.

4 Put the card authorization form, receipt, and guest check into the folder and carry it back to the table. Keep the card with you so you can verify the signature later.

5 Return the card to the actual card owner (not necessarily the person to whom you originally gave the guest check).

6 Leave the table so the guest can complete the tip and sign the card authorization form in private.

7 Watch the table so you know when this has been completed. Do not make the guest sit for more than a minute or two after completion.

8 Return to the table when the guest has signed the card receipt.

9. Verify that the signature on the card receipt matches that on the back of the card.

10. Return the card to the customer.

11. Thank the customer for his or her business and the tip, and complete the remaining goodbye protocol of your operation.

Daily Reconciliation

An important part of ensuring profit is reconciliation, which is the process of matching recorded sales against actual payments received. Guest check payments such as cash, checks, card transactions, or gift certificates are situations involving direct guest contact and, therefore, components of customer service. Credit or debit card reconciliation requires money to be correctly accounted for, including properly allocating servers' tips. Since servers' expectations must be satisfied to ensure high-quality customer service, tip allocation is part of internal customer service.

Also, mistakes can happen in all forms of cash handling, including credit or debit card processing. Therefore, it is important to reconcile daily card transactions with receipts kept by cashiers or servers to compare the dollar value and quantity reported per server code or register closeout.

Handling credit or debit cards is easy if there are no mistakes or fraud. However, that is not always the case. The next section deals with security aspects of handling credit or debit cards.

Think About It...

Have you ever had your credit card or its information stolen? What did you have to do about it?

Security Issues Dealing with Credit or Debit Card Payments

In addition to collecting operational information from credit or debit card transactions, you must also consider security issues. Your operation must have a system for guest credit or debit card security, including:

- Preventing card abuse, such as using an invalid card, someone else's card, a fake card, etc.

- Maintaining the privacy of the guest's personal and financial information.

Point-of-Sale (POS) System

Good POS systems incorporate security into their programming. Two major considerations when choosing a POS system are:

- Whether the first four or last four digits of the credit card or debit card will print on cashier receipts

- Full credit or debit card numbers printing only when management closes out registers

Preventing Credit or Debit Card Abuse

Staff members who handle credit or debit card transactions should be trained on preventing card abuse. Train staff to:

- Check personal identification when taking cards

- Check to see that the card is signed

- Check to see that the signature on the card reasonably matches the signature on the personal identification

- Check that the expiration date has not passed

Handling "Not Approved" Credit or Debit Cards

"Not approved" or "declined" credit or debit cards must be handled with dignity and respect for the guest. The guest should be politely and discreetly informed of the situation and asked for another method of payment. Management should specify how this is done in the operation and include it in the staff training. Staff should also be informed in training that cards are declined for many reasons. For instance, electronic and operator errors are common in the approval process. Many times, a second running of the card will result in an authorization or approval. In the event you do not get approval, consider the guest's feelings and be empathetic when dealing with this type of situation.

Point-of-Sale Issues Affecting Profit

Suggestive selling at the point of sale is an excellent way to increase guest satisfaction and increase profit. As mentioned in Chapter 4, suggestive selling can enhance a guest's dining experience. Suggesting the purchase of gift certificates is a way to satisfy guest desire and can be an additional revenue source.

Think About It...

Consumer transactions are becoming more electronic, and fewer business transactions involve cash. Guests are using credit or debit cards more frequently— even quick-service restaurants now accept credit cards. What impact will this have on payment issues, POS systems, and staff training?

Gift certificates are a form of money and can be redeemed for goods and services as if they were cash. Your establishment must have a policy and procedures on gift certificate sales and redemption. Such a policy might include:

■ **The fixed dollar amounts available for purchase, or variable dollar amounts that can be written on a certificate.**

■ **How long the gift certificate is valid**—This is important because the establishment gets the cash "up front" and has to deliver the goods and services later. Having a large dollar amount in unredeemed gift certificates can make reviewing the profits confusing.

■ **How gift certificate sales should be recorded in your accounting system**—You can consider them as current revenue as of the date of sale or consider them as a debt owed to the certificate holder until it is redeemed. Both methods have accounting implications.

■ **The procedures for redeeming gift certificates**—How to enter them into the POS system and/or your establishment's books depends on how you record their sale.

Exhibit 5e

To-go dining is more popular than ever.

To-Go, Delivery, and Drive-Through Orders

To-go, delivery, and drive-through orders are popular alternative dining methods. (See *Exhibit 5e.*) They bring an opportunity for additional revenue and profit. Also with them come more opportunities for mistakes, abuse, and theft. To ensure customer satisfaction and profitability, the following systems should be in place and consistently followed:

■ POS system that can accommodate these types of sales

■ Staff training on the POS system and procedures for these orders

■ Procedure for confirming orders made via phone, fax, and email

■ Way to get the orders to the kitchen staff

■ Policies and procedures for packaging orders

■ Way to get prepared orders and information about their pickup or delivery to the servers who will package them

■ System for storing and identifying these orders between packaging and delivery or pickup

■ Policies, procedures, and systems for collecting payment for deliveries, including cash, checks, and credit or debit cards

■ Getting delivery money back to the establishment and properly matched to the order in the POS system

■ Procedure to confirm that deliveries were received and drive-through and to-go orders were picked up

Phone, fax, and email technology are driving forces in the popularity of these alternative dining methods. POS systems address the technical aspect of to-go, delivery, and drive-through orders. However, your staff should be properly trained to handle these alternative methods. They should be trained on the above systems and their procedures. They should also have additional skills, such as speaking with customers on the telephone. For example, assigning a designated employee to be responsible for to-go orders can be an effective way to reduce confusion.

Activity

Take Charge

Get a copy of the credit or debit card payment procedure at a local restaurant or foodservice establishment, or review the procedure with the manager. On a separate sheet of paper, write a summary of the procedure and then make suggestions for improvements. In class, participate in a discussion comparing and contrasting the different credit card and debit card payment procedures that were obtained. Complete the discussion by having the class create a credit card and debit card payment procedure.

Summary

Having a system for accepting a variety of payment forms is important to the success of any restaurant or foodservice operation. The payment system should be secure for both the business and the guest. Technology can solve many problems; however, improperly using technology can create new problems. Installing the appropriate system for collecting and recording payments and then properly training the appropriate staff on that system will contribute to satisfied internal and external customers.

Convenience is a growing trend in foodservice. Therefore, to-go, delivery, and drive-through orders are important parts of the sales mix. Proper procedures and training in this area are important to maintaining a competitive edge.

Review Your Learning

1 You can help ensure revenue generation by properly

  A. reporting revenue.

  B. collecting payments.

  C. controlling profits.

  D. fixing prices.

2 Daily reconciliation is important to your operation because it

  A. increases daily revenues.

  B. tracks card payments.

  C. accounts for gift certificates.

  D. accounts for money.

3 Which of the following is an example of an additional revenue source?

  A. Gift cards

  B. Personal checks

  C. Credit cards

  D. Tip allocation

4 Cash overages should be

  A. an accepted part of doing a cash business.

  B. a red flag that something serious may be happening.

  C. considered better than cash shortages.

  D. an indication that you have experienced a "quick change" artist.

5 The use of personal checks is

  A. on the increase in business today.

  B. becoming more risky in business today.

  C. on the decrease in business today.

  D. seldom ever a problem in business today.

6 When establishing a credit or debit card payment policy, you should ensure that

  A. all the card numbers are clearly imprinted on the guest receipt.

  B. only the first and last digits of the card will print on the guest receipt.

  C. none of the card numbers are printed on any receipt.

  D. the card expiration date is imprinted on the receipt.

7 Credit or debit card abuse can be reduced by

  A. keeping both the merchant and guest copies at the operation.

  B. matching the signature on the identification with the signature on the gift certificate.

  C. proper staff training on daily reconciliation.

  D. checking against forms of identification.

8 If a card swiped for payment is "not approved," the employee should

  A. keep the card and call a manager.

  B. cut the card in pieces and return it to the customer.

  C. run the card again and then call the customer service number on the back of the card.

  D. politely return the card and discreetly inform the guest.

continued on next page

Review Your Learning *continued from previous page*

9 A customer pays his lunch check with a $100 bill. The server takes the money to the manager to make change and complete the payment. This is an example of a

A. cash overage.

B. daily reconciliation.

C. cash handling process.

D. line item void.

10 For to-go, delivery, and drive-through orders to be effective,

A. proper receipt and recording systems must be in place.

B. specific staff should be assigned to these areas.

C. POS systems should be modified to accommodate these areas.

D. All of the above

Field Project

Actual Customer Service Procedures

There are various customer service procedures used in restaurant and foodservice operations, and also various claims of providing good customer service. The goal of this project is to evaluate these procedures and claims based on the information in this review guide.

Assignment

1 Develop a list of the restaurant or foodservice operations in your area that have a reputation for providing excellent customer service. You should pursue several methods of determining this, such as:

- ☐ Asking friends and family
- ☐ Examining advertisements in newspapers and telephone books
- ☐ Reading restaurant reviews in newspapers and online

2 Categorize the list by different industry segments; i.e., quick service, full service, fine dining, family dining, etc.

3 Select two or three from each segment for a total of eight to ten operations.

4 Arrange a one-hour interview with the owner or manager of each operation to discuss their methods of providing high-quality customer service.

5 Develop several interview questions to determine whether the standards of high-quality customer service are met by each operation. Provide a copy of the questions to the owners or managers in advance.

6 As you conduct the interview, take detailed notes. Do not hesitate to ask additional questions if you think of them.

7 Take a tour of the different operations and look for factors that might affect their ability to deliver their claims of customer service; also keep in mind what you consider to be high-quality customer service.

8 Analyze what you have learned and draw conclusions about:

- ☐ The level of customer service the restaurant or foodservice operations provide
- ☐ Their ability to live up to their claims
- ☐ Problem areas
- ☐ Changes or improvements you would recommend

9 Prepare a report of your findings, analysis, and conclusions. Discuss the similarities and differences among operations in the same segment and also those in different segments.

Notes

Index